MHQ:
The
Quarterly
Journal
of Military
History

Summer 2004
Volume 16, Number 4

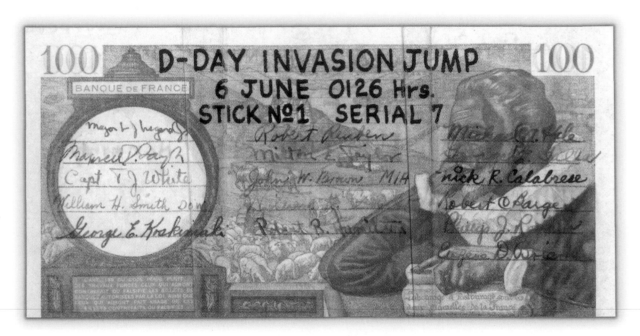

Major General Maxwell Taylor, commander of the 101st Airborne Division, and his "stick"—the troopers assigned to his plane—autographed this one-hundred franc note just before they boarded their C-47 transport to jump into Normandy during the early hours of D-Day. Two members of the stick did not survive the campaign: William H. Smith was fatally injured when he landed, and John W. Brown was killed by a sniper's bullet. John M. Taylor's account of the exploits of the 101st in Normandy begins on page 26 (Courtesy of John M. Taylor).

A NOTE TO OUR READERS

Few American history subjects are more persistently controversial than the way our presidents either enter or initiate major wars. The U.S.–declared War of 1812 created such a furor that delegates from three states met to consider secession from the Union. Some of the Federalists there preposterously claimed that President James Madison was a tool of France. When President James K. Polk opted to fulfill the 1844 Democratic Party platform and extend the United States' borders to the Pacific Ocean, he ordered the U.S. Army to enter Texas and to occupy a disputed area between the Nueces River and Rio Grande. An American detachment there was promptly ambushed by Mexican troops. Upon hearing the news, Polk quickly submitted a budget to support the troops with a preamble that declared a state of war existed. Polk's Whig Party opponents were outraged. They dared not deny aid for the imperiled soldiers, but in voting to support them, they approved a declaration of war. The Whigs, including freshman Congressman Abraham Lincoln, claimed Polk had committed fraud in order to involve America in an immoral war.

Lincoln himself was later accused of deception by the Confederacy's President Jefferson Davis. Davis believed he had been tricked by Lincoln's secretary of state, William Seward, who had promised that Federal troops would evacuate Fort Sumter. Not knowing of Seward's unauthorized statement, Lincoln ordered the fort reinforced. An angry Davis unleashed his military forces on the hapless Federal garrison, and America's bloodiest war began. A similar situation occurred at the outset of the Spanish-American War. In order to gain support from Filipino insurgents against Spain's army in the Philippines, a U.S. consul general, Spenser Pratt, met with the rebel leader, Emilio Aguinaldo. Aguinaldo claimed Pratt promised independence for the Philippines. Realizing that the United States would not honor its pledge, Aguinaldo subsequently led an insurgency against the Americans. Like Lincoln, President William McKinley knew nothing of Pratt's alleged offer.

Accusations continued during the twentieth century. Senator Robert LaFollette revealed that President Woodrow Wilson had ignored his secretary of state's 1915 plea that Wilson should warn Americans about German intentions to destroy any British ship entering the war zone. Wilson had done nothing. The British passenger liner *Lusitania* left New York, 124 U.S. citizens aboard lost their lives in a German torpedo attack, and America tilted toward the British cause. President Franklin D. Roosevelt was the subject of many outlandish charges related to America's entry into World War II, ranging from being an Anglophile to purposely moving the U.S. Pacific Fleet from the comparative safety of Lahaina Roads to the congested anchorage at Pearl Harbor, thereby making the warships a more inviting target. Later, other accusers made convincing claims that the United States contributed to North Korea's and Iraq's decisions to conquer their neighbors—namely, when Secretary of State Dean Acheson, in a January 1950 speech, failed to include South Korea within a defensive perimeter; and when U.S. Ambassador April Glaspie told Saddam Hussein in 1990 that the United States had no opinion on Arab-Arab disputes.

Second-guessing the way America goes to war is almost as old as the republic itself, but no such criticism has been quite as ugly or enduring as the controversy surrounding one of the biggest steps on America's road to full involvement in the Vietnam War—the 1964 Gulf of Tonkin incident. Edward Drea sheds some light on that event beginning on page 74.

Rod Paschall

MHQ: The Quarterly Journal of Military History / Summer 2004

A **PRIMEDIA** Publication

Editor
Rod Paschall

Editorial Director
Roger L. Vance

Associate Editor
Richard G. Latture

Managing Editor
Carl von Wodtke

Senior Editor
Joseph L. Bageant II

Assistant Managing Editor
Nan Siegel

Consulting Editor
Christopher J. Anderson

Creative Director
Barbara Sutliff

Copy Editors
Claudia Gary Annis
Debra R. Newbold
Ellen O'Brien

Art Director
Marty Jones

Editorial Production Coordinator
Beverly D. Frye

Picture Research Director
Gina McNeely

Editorial Resources Coordinator
Shirley M. Bailey

Picture Researcher
Kate Lewin/Paris

Editorial Assistant
Justin Hardy

Picture Research Assistant
Sarah Garner

Contributing Editors
Caleb Carr, David G. Chandler, Theodore F. Cook, Haruko Taya Cook,
Arther Ferrill, Thomas Fleming, Victor Davis Hanson, Alistair Horne,
Samuel Hynes, David Kahn, John Keegan, Paul Kennedy, Richard H. Kohn,
David Clay Large, Jay Luvaas, John A. Lynn, William McNeill, Allan R. Millett,
Williamson Murray, Geoffrey Norman, Robert L. O'Connell, Geoffrey Parker,
H. Darby Perry, Douglas Porch, John Prados, Willard Sterne Randall,
Elihu Rose, Stephen W. Sears, Dennis E. Showalter, Al Silverman,
Ronald H. Spector, Geoffrey C. Ward

Business Manager
Anne Griffin

Lead Production Manager
Karen Johnson

Consumer Marketing Director
Barbara Eskin

Lead Production Planner
Karen M. Bailey

Associate Consumer Marketing Director
Michael Colby

Director, Single Copy Sales
Susan Rose

Associate Consumer Marketing Director
Brian Sullivan

Product Marketing Manager
Bill Breidenstine

PRIMEDIA Lifestyle & Leisure Groups
Senior VP & Group Publishing Director Brent Diamond
VP, Comptroller Stephen H. Bender
VP, Marketing & Internet Operations Dave Evans

PRIMEDIA Consumer Media & Magazine Group
Chief Operating Officer Daniel E. Aks
Executive VP, Consumer Marketing/ Steven Aster
    Circulation
Senior VP/Chief Financial Officer David P. Kirchhoff
Senior VP, Mfg., Production & Distribution Kevin Mullan
Senior VP, Finance Kevin Neary
Senior VP/CIO, Information Technology Debra Robinson
VP, Manufacturing Gregory A. Catsaros
VP, Direct Response & Classified Advertising Carolyn N. Everson
VP, Single Copy Sales Thomas L. Fogarty
VP, Manufacturing Budgets Lilia Golia
    & Operations
VP, Consumer Marketing Christian Dorbandt
VP, Human Resources Kathleen P. Malinowski
VP, Business Development Albert Messina
VP, Database/e-Commerce Suti Prakash

PRIMEDIA Inc.
Chairman Dean Nelson
President & CEO Kelly Conlin
Vice Chairman Beverly C. Chell

PRIMEDIA

Cover: General Dwight D. Eisenhower talks with members of the 502nd Regiment, 101st Airborne Division, about five hours before they jumped into Normandy. A four-article package of D-Day–related stories begins on page 6 (National Archives).

Back cover: Jonathan North describes the 1809 siege of Spanish Saragossa, which was characterized by ferocious street fighting, beginning on page 50 (Achivo Iconografico, S.A./Corbis).

MHQ: The Quarterly Journal of Military History (ISSN 1040-5992) is published quarterly by PRIMEDIA Enthusiast Group. The known office of publication is: 741 Miller Drive SE, Suite D-2, Leesburg, VA 20175. Periodical postage paid at Leesburg, VA, and additional mailing offices. Postmaster: Send subscription information and address changes to: *MHQ*, P.O. Box 420235, Palm Coast, FL 32142-0235. Single copies: $17.99. Yearly subscriptions in U.S.: $74.95; Canada: $84.95; Foreign: $94.95 (in U.S. funds only). *MHQ* neither endorses nor is responsible for the content of advertisements in its pages. Copyright 2003 by PRIMEDIA Enthusiast Group, Inc., a PRIMEDIA Company, all rights reserved. The contents of this magazine may not be reproduced in whole or in part without consent of the copyright owner. *MHQ* is a registered trademark of PRIMEDIA Enthusiast Publications, Inc.

All articles published in *MHQ* are rigorously fact-checked. References for a particular article may be obtained by sending a stamped, self-addressed envelope to our editorial offices. Selected articles are abstracted and indexed in *His-*

Subscription Information:
U.S./Canada: (800) 829-3340
Foreign Subscribers: (386) 447-6318
e-mail: milhistqtl@palmcoastd.com • Web: www.mhqmag.com
Back Issues: (800) 358-6327• (201) 840-4822 (foreign)
Reprints: Contact Wright's Reprints to purchase quality custom reprints or e-prints of articles appearing in this publication at (877) 652-5295, (281) 419-5725 outside the U.S. and Canada.

Canadian Publications Mail Agreement No. 40008153, Return Undeliverable Canadian Addresses to P.O. Box 11, Niagara Falls, ON L2E 6S8
Canadian GST #R123452781

PRINTED IN THE U.S.A.
Canadian GST #R123452781

FLAWED TRIUMPH

AS IN ALL WARS, friction, mistakes, and chance dominated the major battles of World War II, including Normandy. In making all of their decisions, the commanders of the opposing sides in 1944 grappled with uncertainty and ambiguity. Thus, it is not surprising that they would make mistakes. And in the end, those errors would play major roles in the eventual outcome—an overwhelming victory for the Anglo-American Allies. Yet in evaluating those mistakes, one should never underestimate the immense pressures that commanders and their staffs were under throughout the campaign.

The business of history is to understand rather than to condemn. For military commanders confronting the uncertainties of the future, as military historian Sir Michael Howard has suggested, the task is to get it less wrong than their opponents and then to adapt to the conditions as they actually are. In the end, that is precisely what happened for the Allies on D-Day and during the following weeks. The British and the Americans got it less wrong than did the Germans, and they adapted better to the actual conditions they confronted. Nevertheless, the military forces of Nazi Germany were fanatical as well as tactically effective on the battlefield. The eventual Allied victory in Normandy was never a given; it could only have been won by the terrible sacrifices that all too many American, British, Canadian, Polish, and French soldiers were called on to make.

Perhaps the greatest unintended effect of the war was the timing of D-Day itself and the benefit that timing gave to Allied military forces, particularly the Americans. When the United States entered World War II, U.S. Army Chief of Staff General George C. Marshall's preferred approach to the conflict was a "Germany first" strategy that would have seen the Anglo-American powers build up their military forces for a landing on the coast of France in 1943. There would be no peripheral theaters; the United States would have stood on the defensive in the

Pacific. Marshall and his chief planner, Brig. Gen. Dwight D. Eisenhower, fiercely advocated such a strategic approach against Commander in Chief U.S. Fleet Admiral Ernest King, who clearly wanted a "Pacific first" strategy, and against British strategists, who had no desire to get involved on the European continent until the Soviets had further ground down the *Wehrmacht* on the Eastern Front. What Marshall and Eisenhower overlooked was the reality that whatever their strategic analysis might suggest, the American people were not going to tolerate their forces' standing on the defensive in the Pacific—especially after the devastating defeats the Allies had suffered in that theater over the first six months of the war.

For a while in July 1942 it appeared that there would be a strategic impasse because the British were pushing for major Allied operations in the Mediterranean. Their suggestion was to seize French North Africa and open up the Mediterranean to Allied shipping. In the end, President Franklin D. Roosevelt had to step in and order his military advisers to pursue the Mediterranean strategy because the British refused to consider an immediate landing on the French coast. The president may not have realized that Torch, code name for the landings in North Africa, would close off the possibility of a landing on the coast of northwestern Europe in 1943. But he did correctly perceive that if U.S. forces did not act against the Germans in 1942, they might well be entirely pushed into the Pacific first strategy by pressure from the American public, which clearly wanted to bash the Japanese.

Marshall was right that the Torch commitment to the Mediterranean would make a landing on the northwest European coast in the near future impossible. But Roosevelt contended that the commitment of U.S. troops to the Mediterranean theater would help to focus American attention on the war in Europe. The fortuitous effect of all this was that the U.S. Army had a year to pick up hard-learned experience against the

Allied victory in Operation Overlord and the subsequent Battle of Normandy was never a given. In the end, what made the difference was that U.S. and British commanders made fewer grave mistakes than did their German opponents.

By Williamson Murray

Major General Lindsay M. Silvester waves to jubilant French citizens as his 7th Armored Division, Third Army, rolls down a Chartres street on August 16, 1944. By not allowing the Third Army to cross the Seine River and advance to the English Channel, Allied commanders missed a chance to cut off the bulk of German troops in northern France (National Archives).

Wehrmacht. And the Battle of Kasserine Pass underlined how unprepared many of its formations were at the beginning of 1943. But in North Africa the *Wehrmacht* had little chance to take advantage of its initial strike against American forces in the fashion that it would have been able to on the coasts of France in 1943. Consequently, the great Anglo-American landing came on the coasts of France in 1944 with generals and troops far better prepared for the ordeal that was to come—an unintended but perhaps foreseeable consequence of political necessity.

One of the major features of postwar German memoirs was the snide comments by surviving generals on the supposed lack of strategic acumen displayed by Field Marshal Erwin Rommel during the course of the war. Supposedly, the "Desert Fox" was a brilliant divisional commander during the war and a competent though reckless corps commander, but he was most inadequate as a strategist and logistician—the latter two specialties allegedly the purview of the geniuses on the general staff. In fact, that was all sheer and utter nonsense. General staff officers never displayed the slightest understanding of the larger strategic issues in the war, while their astonishingly botched planning for Operation Barbarossa, the invasion of the Soviet Union, takes one's breath away.

On the other hand, Rommel's résumé through 1942 included nothing about strategy and little about logistics. Instead his command—a corps-sized force, as its title *Afrika Korps* suggests—was only responsible for keeping the British from overwhelming the Italians in Libya. He more than achieved that aim. The *Afrika Korps'* lightning-swift strikes, a combination of operational maneuver and tactical defense, consistently rocked the British back on their heels and kept much of their military effort far from Germany's vital interests for more than a year and a half.

But when the British finally gathered together sufficient strength under a competent commander—General Bernard Law Montgomery—Rommel recognized that the game in North Africa was up. Thus, shortly after the *Afrika Korps'* defeat at El Alamein, he recommended that Axis forces be entirely withdrawn from North Africa. He was overruled by not only Hitler but also the general staff officers in the OKW (*Oberkommando der Wehrmacht*—high command of the *Wehrmacht*). The German collapse in Tunisia ensued, which could have had far greater consequences in early summer of 1943 had Allied commanders been willing to take risks by launching amphibious operations more quickly. The Germans had no operational reserves in the Mediterranean theater due to the losses suffered in North Africa.

Top: Field Marshal Erwin Rommel (left) inspects defenses along the Normandy coast. Above: The war is over for this bloodied member of the 12th SS Panzer Division, Hitlerjugend (Hitler Youth). During June fighting around Caen, the 12th SS systematically murdered Canadian prisoners.

In early 1944, Hitler appointed Rommel to energize a lagging effort to prepare the "Atlantic Wall" to meet the expected massive amphibious operation by the Anglo-American armies. Nevertheless, Hitler failed to establish clear lines of authority between Rommel, who was given command of Army Group B with responsibility for the defense of the coastline from Brittany to Germany, and Field Marshal Gerd von Rundstedt, who remained as the overall commander in the West. Moreover, the *Führer* continued to retain personal control of substantial portions of the best divisions in the West, particularly the panzer divisions.

Almost immediately, a major conflict arose between Rommel and von Rundstedt over the operational approach the *Wehrmacht* should take in addressing the invasion threat. That argument had important strategic implications. Rommel argued that in view of the air superiority the Allies would enjoy, the *Wehrmacht* had no choice but to defend forward on the beaches. He was, of course, drawing from his experiences in the bitter battles of North Africa, from El Alamein to Tunisia. If the Western Allies succeeded in making a lodgment on the Continent, Rommel argued, their logistical and air superiority would guarantee that they would win the ensuing race to build up forces. That in turn would inevitably lead to the Reich's defeat.

Von Rundstedt, on the other hand, argued that the German army could not prevent the Allies from making a successful landing. Thus his preferred operational approach was to fight a war of defensive maneuver across northern France back to Germany's frontier. To what end, von Rundstedt never made clear. In effect, his approach was a recipe for defeat; it would only have ensured a higher casualty bill and the destruction of most of northern France, which could only have made the peace terms for Germany that much harsher.

Who had the better sense of the operational and strategic realities? Undoubtedly Rommel. But von Rundstedt's arguments led Hitler to settle on neither approach, so that some of the better divisions moved up toward the coast, but the bulk of the panzer divisions remained well back to launch a counterattack—a dubious approach in view of Allied air superiority. The panzer divisions also remained firmly under Hitler's control. Thus there would be no counterattack against the Allied beachheads during the first hours of the landings, much less days of the campaign.

Moreover, the argument between Rommel on one side and Hitler and von Rundstedt on the other, descended to the tactical level, with pernicius results for German defensive prospects. The Desert Fox had wanted to station the well-equipped 12th

SS Panzer Division, *Hitlerjugend* (Hitler Youth), at Isigny, along the Vire River, barely twelve miles southwest of the area that the Allies had designated Omaha Beach, but Rommel was overruled. In such a position, the young *Waffen* SS troopers would have been able to intervene swiftly in the fighting at either Utah Beach, about eight miles northwest, or Omaha Beach.

These German mistakes in the overall operational thinking and deployments must be counted as among the most disastrous blunders of World War II. They clearly reflected von Rundstedt's and Hitler's fallacious assumptions as to the strength and effectiveness of the coming Allied landings. Nor does the senior German leadership appear to have understood the enormous handicap under which their troops would be operating in the face of Allied air superiority once the invasion began.

the 1st and 29th Infantry Divisions' landings on the beaches, in effect placing the entire D-Day operation in question.

On the tactical level, the German response to the Allied invasion displayed the *Wehrmacht*—army and *Waffen* SS—at its most effective. Throughout June and July, outnumbered German units fought a skillful tactical battle that held the Allies within a tight lodgment in Normandy—one that for that entire period frustrated their efforts to break out. Nevertheless, that very skill would set the stage for one of the great military disasters of World War II. That disaster in turn would be the result of a serious, but understandable, mistake the Allies made in their planning for the Normandy invasion.

Not surprisingly, Anglo-American planning focused on achieving a successful lodgment on the Continent above all else. Allied commanders and planners, however, failed to consider

Rommel argued that in view of the air superiority the Allies would enjoy, the *Wehrmacht* had no choice but to defend forward on the beaches.

With his immense energy, Rommel undertook to ensure that the forces under his command, the Seventh and Fifteenth Armies and the LXXXVIII Corps, would be able to put up the maximum resistance possible along the beach defenses of northern France and the Low Countries. Like the rest of the German military leaders—and most of the time Hitler—he calculated that the most probable landing locations were along the Pas de Calais, an assessment that rested on an underestimation of Allied logistical capabilities. Nevertheless, Rommel put enormous effort into checking and pushing defensive preparations throughout northern France, including the Normandy area. In the Omaha Beach area, the commander of the Seventh Army's 352nd Infantry Division, Maj. Gen. Dietrich Kraiss, had deployed troops between Isigny, in the west, and Arromanches, at the east end of his defensive sector.

The U.S. landings at Omaha Beach would have likely failed if Maj. Gen. Dietrich Kraiss had obeyed Rommel's orders to deploy all his battalions along the coast.

One of the legends of the Normandy campaign is that the Germans stationed the entire 352nd Division along the Omaha Beach landing area unbeknown to Allied intelligence, which believed that the lower-quality 716th Division was manning beach defenses there. Despite the fact that Kraiss possessed ten infantry and five artillery battalions (he also had command of the 716th Division's 726th Regiment), he stationed one-third of his force along the Vire River, kept one whole regiment (the 915th) as a reserve twelve miles inland, assigned two battalions to the defense of the Arromanches area, and left only two battalions along Omaha Beach, one of them a weak holdover from the 716th Division. On several occasions Rommel expressed his unhappiness with Kraiss' dispositions and urged him to move his battalions up to the areas where the Americans would eventually land. Kraiss paid no attention. The general's willful oversight was to play an essential role in enabling the Americans to gain a tenuous foothold at Omaha. Had Kraiss followed Rommel's directions, the Germans would have undoubtedly defeated

sufficiently the nature of the terrain that lay behind the beaches—the *bocage* country, a region of France typified by narrow lanes, high hedgerows with root systems built up over the millennia separating small fields, and farmhouses and barns built out of heavy regional stones. The whole area would prove a defender's paradise—especially when that defender was as skilled in defensive tactics as were the Germans. Thus almost immediately after the Allies had created their successful lodgment and linked the various beaches together, they discovered themselves in a nightmarish battle of attrition in which forward movement was slow and costly, bought with the blood of Allied soldiers. In every respect the Norman countryside played to German strength at the tactical level.

The one Allied commander who might have made a significant difference, because he knew the Norman countryside, was unfortunately in England, whiling away his time leading an imaginary army the British had created to threaten a landing on the Pas de Calais. Lieutenant General George S. Patton was paying the price for having slapped two shell-shocked American soldiers in a hospital in Sicily—particularly galling in that he had to watch Lt. Gen. Omar Bradley wage an unimaginative campaign over the first two months of the fighting in France. Patton knew the Norman countryside because he had traveled over it extensively just before World War I—eerily in the belief that he would eventually fight on that same ground. He would get his chance at the end of the Normandy campaign, but the initial difficulties of fighting in the *bocage* country would be handled by others far less skilled than he.

Yet, ironically, the effect of the Allied lack of preparation and difficulties in fighting in the hedgerow countryside may have benefited the campaign's eventual outcome. For all their tactical skill on the defensive, the Germans were fighting a battle

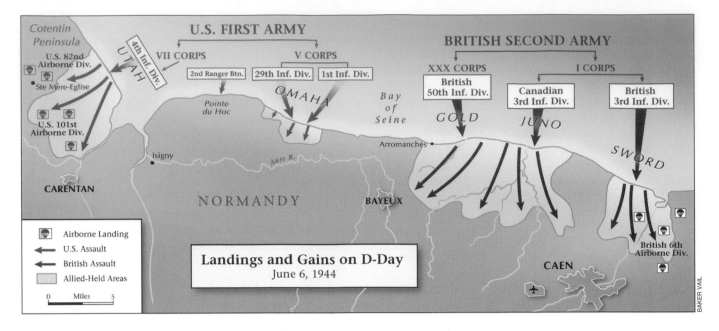

Cotentin Peninsula

U.S. 82nd Airborne Div.

Ste Mère-Eglise

U.S. 101st Airborne Div.

CARENTAN

NORMANDY

Isigny

Pointe du Hoc

Aure R.

U.S. FIRST ARMY

4th Inf. Div.

VII CORPS

V CORPS

UTAH

2nd Ranger Btn.

29th Inf. Div.

1st Inf. Div.

OMAHA

Bay of Seine

BAYEUX

BRITISH SECOND ARMY

XXX CORPS

I CORPS

British 50th Inf. Div.

Canadian 3rd Inf. Div.

British 3rd Inf. Div.

Arromanches

GOLD

JUNO

SWORD

British 6th Airborne Div.

CAEN

Legend:
- Airborne Landing
- U.S. Assault
- British Assault
- Allied-Held Areas

0   Miles   5

Landings and Gains on D-Day
June 6, 1944

BAKER VAIL

that in the end played to Allied strengths. The relentless air campaign against the transportation network of northern France that had begun in early April ensured that the Allies would win the battle of the buildup, even when a savage Atlantic storm—one of the worst of the century—destroyed one of the artificial Mulberry harbors through which supplies were flowing to British and U.S. armies. On one hand, German divisions moving to the Normandy theater had to contend with smashed bridges, bombed-out road crossings, and continual Allied air attacks along French roads. There would be no help from the French railroads. The 2nd *Waffen* SS Division, *Das Reich*, took two weeks, instead of the scheduled two days, to reach the Normandy battlefield from its cantonment areas near Limoges due to the difficulties it encountered in moving forward through areas controlled by Allied fighter-bombers and the French Resistance. Meanwhile, Allied forces flowed from the sea almost seamlessly into the slowly growing lodgment.

The logistical parameters of the fight were equally grim from the German point of view. Throughout the Battle of Normandy, ammunition and supplies were short, as the *Wehrmacht*'s logistical system struggled to keep frontline units equipped. Their situation might have been worse had the Germans not had access to the Seine River, but they were able to keep a substantial traffic of barges moving down the river at night; Allied air forces failed to give the river traffic the attention they gave the French rail and road networks. Thus *Wehrmacht* logisticians found it easier to supply the eastern side of the Normandy battlefield than the western, and that fact may help to explain why the German line finally broke in western Normandy rather than in the east.

In the final analysis, the fighting in Normandy was precisely the kind of battle that best suited the capabilities of Montgomery, the Allied ground commander, and those of his soldiers, American as well as British. The troubles Allied forces experienced early in the fighting again suggest that a battle of maneuver on German terms might well have led to some considerable setbacks. Montgomery's initial plans had called for British forces to drive through and capture Caen on D-Day.

Control of Normandy's capital would then, as he argued in his memoirs, have allowed the British to fight a mobile battle in the more open countryside to the east and southeast of Caen. In fact, such a battle would not at all have been to the advantage of British troops.

In retrospect, it was fortunate that British and Canadian forces did not capture Caen on the invasion's first day. On June 7 they had a difficult enough time in holding onto their positions in the desperate fighting that ensued when the *Hitlerjugend* Panzer Division arrived on the battlefield. ("Hitler's Murderers" would have been a better name for the division, for its members systematically killed more than 150 Canadian soldiers captured during the fighting in Normandy.) The failure to achieve Montgomery's goals therefore placed Canadian and British troops in a more favorable position to defend themselves against the initial German counterattacks. Moreover, because they were closer to the shore, it was easier to call in naval gunfire support, which in the early days of the campaign often proved a devastating plus for Allied ground troops.

The disaster at Villers-Bocage on June 13 underlines how unprepared the British were to conduct a mobile battle against the Germans. In effect a whole brigade of the 7th Armored Division outflanked the German defenses at Caen and swept into the crossroads town of Villers-Bocage. But, just as they were in position to unhinge German defenses in Normandy, disaster struck. In one of the most calamitous tactical failures of the Normandy campaign, the British were not deployed in tactical, battle formation. A small group of German Tiger tanks, under the command of panzer ace Lt. Col. Michael Wittmann, then managed to destroy much of the British force—including twenty-seven Cromwell, Sherman Firefly, and Stuart tanks—and send the rest scurrying back to their starting line. The commander of the British Second Army, Lt. Gen. Miles Dempsey, acidly commented after the defeat, "The whole handling of that battle was a disgrace." Under no circumstance were the British prepared to fight a truly mobile battle against the Germans.

Lest an American audience become too smug, one should

Although Allied planning for the D-Day landings was meticulous, U.S. and British commanders failed to sufficiently consider the Norman countryside behind the beaches, marked by narrow lanes (left), large hedgerows (right), and stone farmhouses—perfect defensive ground.

not forget that the performance of some U.S. units in the first days of the campaign was less than stirring. The future general William Dupuy, an officer in the 90th Infantry Division when it landed in Normandy, once described his division as the finest machine for killing Americans ever invented. So bad was the 90th's performance that Eisenhower and Bradley for a time considered breaking it up entirely and parceling its men and their equipment out to other divisions.

The result of the slugging match was that Allied military operations in June and July slowly but steadily ground the Germans down to the breaking point. The Allied offensives—Charnwood, Goodwood, and Montgomery's other attacks on the eastern flank of the Normandy lodgment—were anything but imaginative. In the west, Bradley's First Army, reflecting the uninspired leadership of its commander, launched a series of broad, division-sized attacks that possessed neither the firepower nor the combat punch to break through the German lines. As a number of German observers noted after the war, there was simply no *Schwerpunkt*—focal point might be the best translation—to the American attacks. Across the front, the *Wehrmacht* bent and at times pulled back, but did not break. Yet their frontline formations were steadily ground into the dirt, while few soldiers arrived from rear areas to replace the mounting casualties. Day after day, German losses in men and equipment mounted, but with defeats swallowing up *Wehrmacht* forces on all fronts, there were simply no reinforcements for them.

PERHAPS THE MOST astonishing error of the Normandy campaign—an error of truly monumental proportions because it affected virtually all the battles conducted between the Anglo-American Allies and the Germans throughout World War II— was Germany's arrogant overconfidence in the security of its system for encoding radio messages, which utilized Enigma encryption

Germany's greatest blunder of the war was overconfidence in the security of its system for encoding top-secret radio messages, which utilized the Enigma encryption machine (above).

machines. In fact, British code-breakers, with the help of the Poles, had managed crack the *Wehrmacht*'s highest-grade ciphers during the first year of the war. Yet, despite innumerable demonstrations that the Western Allies seemed to possess a sixth sense about German military operations, the *Wehrmacht*'s senior leaders never seem to have suspected that their opponents were reading their most highly classified secrets.

Not surprisingly, there were situations in which that advantage played a significant role in the Allied conduct of operations in Normandy. Ultra, the information gleaned from decrypts of German message traffic, would prove highly useful to Allied commanders. Code-named Fortitude, the whole deception campaign to persuade the Germans that the main Allied landings would occur on the beaches of the Pas de Calais rested on insights Ultra provided on the German high command. Before a German counterattack landed at Mortain in early August, Ultra provided the crucial early warning. And early in June, Ultra decrypts had indicated where Panzer Group West, under General Leopold Geyr von Schweppenburg, was establishing its headquarters. Allied fighter-bombers soon swooped in to destroy the headquarters, many of its vehicles, and a substantial number of staff officers. Panzer Group West would, as a result, never become an operational headquarters. The fact that the Germans had established its location in open fields indicates that some German ground commanders were not yet aware of what Allied air superiority in the West meant. It also suggests that Allied fighter aircraft likely would have eventually located it even without Ultra's help.

Ultra intelligence by itself was never to prove decisive, because in the end the Allies had to dig the Germans out of their trenches and defensive positions. It might suggest what enemy intentions might be or the order that German forces were arriving on the battlefield, but the killing zone still had to be crossed and the enemy defeated. The Germans nevertheless fought the Normandy campaign with their operational concepts and the disposition of most of their forces fully exposed to the prying eyes and ears of Allied decryption efforts. The German leadership's blind confidence in their encryption system for radio traffic was indeed an error of monumental proportions.

The Allied break came with stunning suddenness at the end of July. The Americans had finally learned many of the tactical and operational lessons from the fighting thus far. In one ingenious example of the former, they had figured out how to weld portions of the girders that had formed German beach obstacles onto the front of Sherman tanks. Thus equipped, the Shermans could cut right through the root systems that held *bocage* hedgerows in place. The Americans were then able to achieve a cross-country mobility that the Germans could not match.

positions. Bombing perpendicular to the front, creep-back resulted in even greater fratricide, this time killing 121 Americans, including Lt. Gen. Leslie McNair, and wounding 490.

But however great the damage to American troops was, the damage to German frontline positions was even more devastating. In fact, the fratricide may well have ensured that all of those positions got thoroughly plastered, along with the defenses farther back. The commander of the *Panzer Lehr* Division, Maj. Gen. Fritz Bayerlein, reported to his superiors: "Out in front everyone is holding out. Everyone. My grenadiers and my engineers and my tank crews—they're holding their ground. Not a single one is leaving his post. They are lying silent in their foxholes for they are dead."

Initially, the Americans failed to make a clean breakthrough. Feeling that the German line was about to crack, Collins nevertheless launched his armor before his initial wave had broken

'Out in front everyone is holding out....Not a single one is leaving his post. They are lying silent in their foxholes for they are dead.'

Even more important, Bradley finally concentrated his forces for an attack, code-named Operation Cobra, aimed at achieving a breakthrough. Under the leadership of one of the most competent corps commanders in the U.S. Army, Maj. Gen. J. Lawton Collins, VII Corps struck on a front of only seven thousand yards. The Eighth Air Force's heavy bombers were to open up the offensive with a massive bombing of the German forward positions. On July 24 the planes had been recalled because of weather, but a number of them dropped their loads anyway, and bombs that landed short killed twenty-five Americans and wounded 131. Bradley had asked that the bombers attack parallel to the front to lessen the chance of fratricide. The Eighth's commanders decided otherwise, and on July 25 one thousand heavies and their accompanying fighters plastered the German

GIs, hammered at the beginning of Operation Cobra by U.S. bombs that fell short, dig themselves out before advancing. After weeks of attritional fighting in Normandy, U.S. Lt. Gen. Omar Bradley had concentrated his forces for a breakthrough battle. Allied bombers softened up German defenses for the ground attack made by Maj. Gen. J. Lawton Collins' VII Corps.

through the remaining German defenses. Thus, when Bayerlein's forward positions crumbled, American armor was in a position to take full advantage of the German collapse.

Collins immediately recognized that this was the opening for which American forces had been waiting. Despite Bradley's hesitancy, Collins drove his corps straight through Coutances, Cérences, and La Haye-Pesnel down Normandy's west coast toward Avranches. In effect, the U.S. advance forced the Germans away from the coast and created a long, relatively thin penetration. Once that drive reached Avranches, the Americans would have a clear path in a number of directions: northeast into the Brittany Peninsula, directly south to cut the peninsula off, and southeast to curve back behind the enemy's lines to take the *Wehrmacht* in Normandy in the rear—perhaps to envelop the German military's entire force in the West and win one of the greatest victories of World War II. At that point both sides were to make a series of operational errors that in the end lengthened the war into 1945 and extended the killing for another six months.

Unfortunately, but understandably for such prospects, Allied senior commanders had been focusing over the past two months on creating a breakthrough. No one, except perhaps Patton, had been contemplating what to do after a breakthrough had occurred. The result was that the first reaction to Cobra's success, as American divisions roared up to and through Avranches, was to resurrect the pre–D-Day plan, which had called for an advance into Brittany to seize ports there. The aim of preinvasion planning was to lighten the logistical load that the Normandy beaches might have to carry into the winter. The problem with such an approach was twofold. The port demolitions that the Germans had conducted in Cherbourg indicated that even when the Allies captured the Bretton ports, they were going to be useless for the foreseeable future. Futhermore, any advance into Brittany would take the American forces to the west, away from the Norman battlefields, where the German western flank was now entirely up in

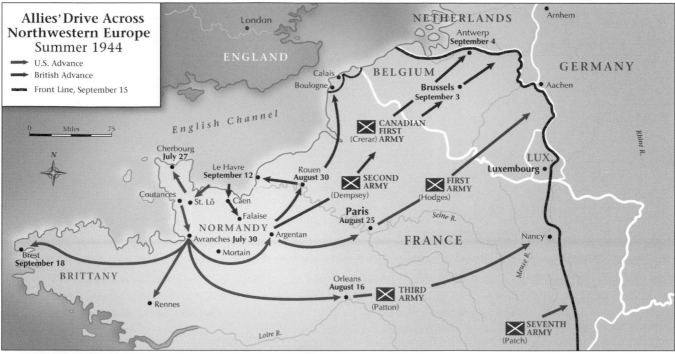

**Allies' Drive Across
Northwestern Europe
Summer 1944**

→ U.S. Advance
→ British Advance
▬ Front Line, September 15

0   Miles   75

N

English Channel

London
ENGLAND

NETHERLANDS
Arnhem
Antwerp
September 4
BELGIUM
Calais
Boulogne
Brussels
September 3
GERMANY
Aachen

Cherbourg
July 27
Le Havre
September 12
Rouen
August 30
CANADIAN
FIRST
(Crerar) ARMY
LUX.
Luxembourg
Rhine R.

Coutances
St. Lô
Caen
Falaise
SECOND
ARMY
(Dempsey)
FIRST
ARMY
(Hodges)

NORMANDY
Avranches July 30
Argentan
Paris
August 25
Seine R.
FRANCE
Nancy

Brest
September 18
Mortain
Meuse R.

BRITTANY

Rennes
Orleans
August 16
THIRD
ARMY
(Patton)
SEVENTH
ARMY
(Patch)

Loire R.

BAKER VAIL

Once a breakthrough was achieved, Allied leaders committed an operational mistake by falling back on a pre–D-Day plan to liberate Breton ports. American troops thus headed west into Brittany (above) and away from the Germans' exposed flank in Normandy.

U.S. ARMY

the air. Bradley nevertheless clung to the plan.

By then Patton had arrived on the scene and was actively participating in operations. He would soon take over a newly created entity, the Third Army. The hard-hitting general sensed that an enormous opportunity was in the offing. He also realized, however, just how tenuous his position was with his immediate superiors: General Eisenhower had made it clear that he would not stand for another "incident," while Bradley, ever jealous of a subordinate who was his superior in terms of the art of command, could hardly wait to fire Patton. Thus, when Maj. Gen. John Wood, commander of the 4th Armored Division—one of the first divisions through Avranches and into the open—protested his orders to head west, Patton sympathized but refused to make waves. The 4th and 6th Armored, the first two U.S. divisions in the breakout, therefore headed due west—entirely away from the inviting area to the south and east.

BRADLEY FINALLY WOKE UP, and Patton, as of August 1 commander of the Third Army, was allowed to turn the next corps through Avranches to the south and east. That move immediately threatened German supply dumps in Normandy and in the long term all the German forces in western France.

Hitler's baleful influence then directly affected German operations in the West and presented the Allies with more opportunities. Looking at the narrow corridor running from St. Lô in the north to Avranches at the southwest corner of Normandy, the *Führer* decided that a determined counterattack would cut off the American breakthrough and restore the situation in Normandy. Hitler overruled the commanders on the scene, who argued that such a plan could not succeed in the face of Allied air superiority.

What appeared on the maps in the *Führer*'s headquarters to be an enticing opportunity, however, was in fact something quite different in reality. The terrain through which a German

Faced with the breakout, Adolf Hitler blundered by ordering a concentrated counterattack to restore the front line in Normandy. The U.S. Army was ready, however, and during fighting around Mortain (left) it halted the German drive. The Allies then fumbled an opportunity to bag all of the surviving enemy troops by failing to quickly close the Falaise Gap. Right: Wrecked German armor litters a road north of Mortain.

counterattack would run was the same sort of countryside that had enabled the *Wehrmacht* to hold the Allied forces back in June and July. Moreover, Avranches itself sat high on a hill that dominated the surrounding countryside, and from which Americans could call in artillery and fighter strikes. Similarly, a number of prominent terrain features near Mortain would also allow the U.S. forces to dominate any enemy action in the area. Finally, in order to launch such a counterattack the Germans would have to shift substantial forces to the west, thereby increasing their chances of being trapped by the Americans and British there.

At this point in the war, with the failure of the July 20 plot to assassinate Hitler, no German general, much less Field Marshal Günther von Kluge—who had succeeded von Rundstedt as commander in the West and had himself been involved in the plot—was going to risk the *Führer*'s wrath by arguing against his orders. Thus, as the Third Army began to drive east, German forces moved deeper into an already forming pocket. Almost immediately Ultra intelligence revealed German intentions to launch a major counterattack aimed at breaking through to the Atlantic and cutting off U.S. forces that had broken through. Hitler had set the stage for what might have been one of the greatest victories in American military history. Bradley, with help from Eisenhower and Montgomery, now proceeded to bungle the opportunity.

By using reserve divisions that were arriving in the theater, von Kluge managed to cobble together four panzer divisions to launch Hitler's westward strike. The U.S. 30th Infantry Division did a masterful job in blunting the German attacks by controlling the hills in the Mortain area. This meant that German armor on the low ground had no chance. Particularly noteworthy was the performance of the 2nd Battalion, 120th Infantry Regiment, with all four company commanders earning Distinguished Service Crosses.

Patton's armored divisions, meanwhile, were throwing an encircling arm around German forces in Normandy. On August 11, Montgomery took the first step toward failure by ordering that Argentan would remain the boundary line between his forces driving southward and the Americans driving northward. The British, however, had not yet reached Falaise, while the Americans were already at Argentan. Moreover, the British Second Army attacking from the north still had substantial enemy forces in front of them, including the remains of the 12th SS, while no German forces were in front of the Americans.

Only Patton sensed the opportunity. On the evening of August 12, he urged Bradley to let him push Maj. Gen. Wade Haislip's XV Corps all the way to Falaise, which would have completed the encirclement of German forces. Bradley issued an obdurate refusal without even bothering to consult with Montgomery. After the war he would blame Montgomery for the failure to close the gap, but in fact he was even more at fault. Bradley simply refused to grasp the opportunity—probably due to his deep jealousy of his subordinate, Patton. As the British advance slowly ground forward and increasing numbers of Germans escaped through what became known as the Falaise Gap, Bradley continued to procrastinate.

On August 17, Patton suggested that his forces, already well on the way to the Seine, cross that river and then sweep up to the Channel to put the escaping Germans as well as a portion of the German Fifteenth Army in the bag. Again he received a decisive no in reply. The problem was that neither Montgomery nor Bradley understood that the name of the operational game at this point in the war was the destruction of enemy armies, as the Soviets had so decisively demonstrated in their decimation of Army Group Center during Operation Bagration in June and July of that year. Instead, like World War I generals, the Allied high command focused on gaining territory. In addition, it appears that Montgomery was already focusing on his completely wrong-headed idea that the way to beat Germany in 1944 was to give him complete control of Allied armies in order to launch a massive drive straight through to the north German plain. He took his eyes off the battle in front of him as he dreamed of possibilities that quite simply were not in the cards.

The failure of the Allies to close off the Falaise Gap in the period between August 13 and 20 allowed the Germans to extract more than fifty thousand of their best troops from the collapse in the West. Equally important, they were also able to extricate the staffs of a number of their divisions and corps. Those organizations were to prove crucial as the Germans reknit their defenses along the Third Reich's frontier and brought the Allied advance to a decisive halt in September. Without those troops and staffs, it is doubtful whether the Germans could have held the Allies back from a breakthrough at least to the Reich, whatever the Allied logistical difficulties. Such a success would in turn have probably led the Soviets to begin their offensive against German forces in the East earlier than January 1945. But all of that is idle speculation in the face of the failure to close off and complete what should have been the sure destruction of much of the German forces in the West.

While Third Army commander Lt. Gen. George S. Patton (left) realized that the Allies' top priority should be the destruction of German armies, his superiors Bradley (center) and Twenty-first Army Group commander General Bernard L. Montgomery (right) focused on gaining territory.

DURING THE LAST half of August and into early September, Anglo-American forces swept across northern France and on into the Low Countries, thus gathering up the territorial fruits of the German collapse in Normandy. But at the Reich's frontier, their drive ran out of steam, largely as a result not only of their short-term logistical difficulties, but their long-term ones as well. The Allies' advance had in effect placed them on the other side of the transportation desert that their air forces had created to support the Normandy landings. Quite simply, the railroads in western and central France were no longer capable of supporting even minimal forces, while, as Patton was soon to discover, transport trucks required so much fuel they could carry only minimal supplies if they were to get back to the Normandy beaches, where materiel was arriving. The Bretton ports were no help at all.

The key to further operations was supposed to be the greatest port in Western Europe, Antwerp, which the British captured in completely undamaged condition in early September (story P. 36). But neither Montgomery nor his subordinate commanders did anything to open up the Scheldt Estuary, upon which the use of Antwerp depended. Instead, Montgomery focused on the terribly flawed Operation Market-Garden, which not only failed but also ended up delaying the opening of the Scheldt until late November, perhaps the greatest error an Allied commander was to make in 1944.

The Allies might have been in a desperate situation except for the fact that as part of the overall strategy for 1944 the U.S. Joint Chiefs of Staff, with the full backing of President Roosevelt, had forced the British to accept an Allied landing in southern France. The American argument had been that the Allies would need such a landing to help clear the Germans out of southern France and establish a front line running across northern France from Switzerland to the Channel. The British, however, had argued that a French Riviera landing would weaken Allied operations in northern Italy. At least from Churchill's point of view, that would hamper the possibility of conducting military operations in the northern Balkans and perhaps even onto the Hungarian plain. In retrospect, such strategic aims were idle nonsense, Churchill and his chief military adviser, Field Marshal Sir Alan Brooke, at their worst.

An even more important result of the landings in southern France would play a major, but largely unintended, role in the campaign in northern Europe: The capture of Marseilles proved a logistic godsend to the supply of U.S. forces in the fall and early winter of 1944-45. As with Antwerp, the Germans failed to carry out extensive demolitions of Marseilles' port facilities. But equally important was the fact the Allied air attacks on the French transportation network had targeted little of the system that ran from Marseilles up the Rhône River valley. Thus, French railroads, using that route, were able to supply more than 40 percent of the needs of Allied armies on the Western Front through the remainder of 1944. Without that support and with Montgomery's failure to open up the Scheldt and Antwerp until November, Allied armies might not have been able to hold their positions along the German frontier in 1944.

When all is said and done, the Normandy campaign and the subsequent drive across France was a great success. On balance the Allies made fewer grave mistakes than did their opponents. They missed some glowing opportunities in August to destroy German armies, but then perhaps the very nature of the Anglo-American alliance made such failures inevitable. Nor should one ignore the fact that British military power was at the limit of what that nation could support, while the United States was also sustaining a great war in the Pacific. Moreover, while the course of the campaign in France is clear to us at the start of the twenty-first century, what was to happen remained uncertain and ambiguous to those charged with waging war against the unfortunately all-too-effective forces of Nazi Germany. In the end, the Western powers triumphed and by so doing established the essential strategic and political preconditions for the successful conduct of the Cold War. It was in the tragic nature of life and in the fact that no general can ever make perfect decisions that victory in Europe would not come until May 1945.

WILLIAMSON MURRAY is an *MHQ* contributing editor and co-author with Allan R. Millett of *A War to Be Won: Fighting the Second World War* (Belknap Press, 2001), and with Robert H. Scales Jr. of *The Iraq War: A Military History* (Harvard University Press, 2003).

Luftwaffe
MISSING
IN ACTION

by James S. Corum

Poor strategic and tactical decisions and a lack of aircraft and adequately trained pilots helped doom German air operations against the Normandy invasion.

Above right: Wreckage from a Junkers Ju-88 bomber shot down in February 1944 litters a field in Kent, England. Horrendous aircraft losses during an ill-advised terror-bombing offensive against Britain and in defense of German airspace helped render the Luftwaffe incapable of contesting the skies over France in June 1944. Background: The Normandy coast, as seen from an Allied plane.

The most enduring image of the *Luftwaffe*'s reaction to the Allied landings in Normandy on June 6, 1944, comes from a movie, *The Longest Day*. Ordered to respond to the invasion, Lieutenant Colonel Josef "Pips" Priller, commander of *Jagdgeschwader* 26, takes off with his entire available force—himself and one wingman—in their Focke Wulf Fw-190s. Priller and his partner, Heinz Wodarczyk, make one ineffectual strafing run over Sword Beach, then run like hell for home to evade the overwhelming Allied fighter cover. Laughing sardonically, the German ace comments, "Another great victory for the *Luftwaffe*!"

Unlike so many movie depictions of aerial warfare, this one is quite true. In many respects, this scene is characteristic of the *Luftwaffe*'s response on the morning of the invasion, but it is scarcely the whole story. In reality, in the days and weeks after D-Day, the German air force mounted a major campaign against the Allied invasion.

Luftwaffe forces in France and the Low Countries came under the command of *Luftflotte* (Air Fleet) 3, which in June 1944 had 408,598 troops and laborers under its command: 323,139 officers and men of the regular *Luftwaffe*; 16,109 *Helferinen*, uniformed women assigned to the *Luftwaffe*; 45,331 German and foreign workers; and 24,019 Reich Labor Service workers. The forces were organized into several major commands. The X *Fliegerkorps* (Flying Corps), based in southern France, consisted of heavy bombers and naval-attack aircraft. The IX *Fliegerkorps* was a conventional bomber force, mostly made up of twin-engine Junkers Ju-88s. The II *Jagdkorps* (Fighter Corps) was the headquarters for the fighter wings serving in Belgium and France, while *Luftflotte* 3's few fighter-bombers and ground-attack aircraft were organized in the II *Fliegerkorps*. The 3rd's largest command, the III Flak Corps, included tens of thousands of *Luftwaffe* personnel manning radar and flak positions from the Low Countries into France.

Field Marshal Hugo Sperrle, commander of *Luftflotte* 3, was one of the *Luftwaffe*'s most experienced fliers and had long been established among Germany's top air commanders. Sperrle began his aviation career prior to World War I. After earning a distinguished flying record in the Great War, he led the *Luftwaffe*'s Condor Legion in Spain in 1936-37 and *Luftflotte* 3 during the 1940 conquest of France and the Battle of

Britain. Sperrle was highly respected as an experienced and competent leader, but he was also famous for his appearance. More than six feet tall and weighing in at about three hundred pounds, at times he could even make *Luftwaffe* Commander in Chief Hermann Göring appear trim. The scar down his face and his perpetual scowl were accent-

ed by the monocle that he habitually wore. His looks belied a fairly genial nature and a love of high living that was well known in the *Wehrmacht*.

Sperrle's senior commanders in 1944 were as competent and experienced as their Allied counterparts; in fact, it would have been hard to find a group of air officers with more impressive combat records. The X *Fliegerkorps* was commanded by forty-six-year-old Lt. Gen. Alexander Holle, a specialist in anti-shipping operations who had earned the Knight's Cross. Forty-nine-year-old Lt. Gen. Werner Junck, a World War I ace who had served as fighter commander of *Luftflotte* 3 during the Battle of Britain, led the II *Jagdkorps*. The II *Fliegerkorps* was led by fifty-two-year-old Lt. Gen. Alfred Bülowius, who had commanded Battle Group North of the *Luftwaffe* Don Command on the Eastern

In 1943 Field Marshal Hugo Sperrle (above left), commander of Luftflotte 3, *with responsibility for German air operations in the West, advocated a bombing campaign against Allied shipping, but was overruled by Adolf Hitler and* Luftwaffe *Commander in Chief Hermann Göring (top). Above right: Given the title Attack Leader England, Major General Dietrich Peltz (left) led the bombing campaign against British cities.*

Front. Major General Dietrich Peltz, at thirty-two, commanded the IX *Fliegerkorps*. His rapid rise to high rank was due to an especially impressive war record. A bomber and dive-bomber specialist, Peltz had served as a bomber group commander in 1941-42. He later was inspector of the bomber and dive-bomber branch of the *Luftwaffe*. In September 1943, Peltz was promoted to command of the IX *Fliegerkorps*. The III Flak Corps was led by *General der Flakartillerie* Wolfgang Pickert, who had established an outstanding combat record on the Russian Front in 1942-43.

The state of the *Luftwaffe*'s forces in France and Western Europe in 1944 did not approach the quality of its operational leadership, and by late spring the various *Luftflotte* 3 commands were in terrible shape. Air superiority over Germany had been lost in February and March, during massive Allied bombing offensives that featured long-range fighter escorts. The ranks of German pilots were so decimated that in February the *Luftwaffe* began losing more trained pilots than it could replace. By March, 22 percent of Reich air defense pilots had been lost. By April the figure had reached 38 percent and 24 percent of *Luftflotte* 3 pilots were out of action. In April alone, the *Luftwaffe* lost 489 fighter pilots but trained only 396.

To make matters worse, the replacements coming on line were scarcely trained compared with pilots who had learned their craft early in the war. From 1939 to September 1942, *Luftwaffe* fighter and bomber pilots received thorough basic flight training and a course in the latest aircraft models before they were transferred to a combat unit. By late '42, shortages of fuel and instructors resulted in a drastic reduction of pilot training courses, and by mid-'44, *Luftwaffe* fighter pilots were going into action with little more than 130 hours' total aircraft training, of which approximately twenty-five hours was in operational aircraft. In contrast, during that same period fighter pilots of the U.S. Army Air Forces (USAAF) entered combat with well over four hundred hours of flying time, including more than one hundred hours in operational aircraft.

German bomber forces were in even worse shape than fighter units. The former had also suffered heavy attrition and were unable to replace experienced aircrews with pilots and crews of even minimal competence. Bomber units had been steadily decimated after the Soviets trapped the German Sixth Army at Stalingrad in late 1942. The equivalent of three experienced bomber wings were destroyed during the *Luftwaffe*'s attempt to use the large planes to airlift supplies to the besieged and doomed troops. In 1943 bomber units were slowly rebuilt, and the IX *Fliegerkorps*, *Luftflotte* 3's main bomber force, was steadily reinforced. That year Sperrle proposed that the *Luftwaffe*'s bomber units in the West be used in a naval air campaign to attack Allied shipping in and out of Britain from outside of Royal Air Force (RAF) Fighter Command's effective defensive range, rather than in retaliatory attacks on British cities.

Adolf Hitler and Göring emphatically rejected the proposed strategy and ordered a terror-bombing campaign against British cities. Since the Allied bombing of Hamburg in the summer of 1943, the Nazi leadership had turned more and more to terror-bombing campaigns as a strategic weapon. One must remember the enormous importance that propaganda—both against the enemy populace and toward Germany's population—played in the Nazi leaders' concept of war. Hitler and his entourage believed that terror bombing would break British morale and that German home front morale, which was being badly battered by the Allied bombing campaign, would be bolstered by news that British civilians were dying and suffering in the same way that German civilians were.

The *Luftflotte* 3 commander, however, believed the costly attacks were strategically meaningless.

Because of the clash between Sperrle's and Hitler and Göring's strategies, the IX *Fliegerkorps* was effectively taken out of the operational control of *Luftflotte* 3 in the summer of 1943. That fall Peltz was given the title *Angriffsführer* England (Attack Leader England) and placed under the direct command of Göring, who would select the targets for the bomber force. The air corps received substantial reinforcements, both aircrews and bombers, and by December 1943 it consisted of 524 bombers, mostly Ju-88s and Dornier Do-217s, as well as some Heinkel He-177s. Although the force was impressive on paper, there had been no time to train the crews in the night flying and bombing tactics necessary to hit their targets. Göring ordered Peltz to begin a major bombing offensive against British cities as soon as possible, and, against the advice of *Luftflotte* 3, London—the city

Above: Focke Wulf Fw-190Fs were among World War II's best ground-attack aircraft, but in June 1944, poorly trained pilots and overwhelming Allied air superiority curtailed their effectiveness (USAF).

with Britain's largest concentration of anti-aircraft and night-fighter defenses—was selected as the primary target.

Results were expected immediately, and on January 21, 1944, Peltz led a force of 447 bombers on the first big German raid of the new bombing offensive against the capital. The IX *Fliegerkorps'* campaign against British cities, which lasted from January to May 1944, can be rated as one of the most disastrous *Luftwaffe* offensives of World War II. Due to poor training and the lack of effective pathfinders, only a few of the bombs dropped during the campaign came even close to their planned targets. In twenty-nine night attacks, the IX *Fliegerkorps* flew 4,251 sorties. The loss rate averaged 7.7 percent of the force per raid, and by May 1944, 329 bombers and their aircrews had been lost over England. In short, the *Luftwaffe's* largest bomber force destroyed itself in attacks that gained Germany nothing. By D-Day the IX *Fliegerkorps* had only 261 twin-engine bombers, no more than 50 percent of which were operational.

The other *Luftflotte* 3 bomber force, the X *Fliegerkorps*, was in no better shape. It specialized in anti-shipping attacks using torpedoes and radio-guided dive bombs—Fritz Xs and Henschel Hs-293s. Considerable aircrew training was required for these revolutionary weapons—the precision-guided bombs of World War II—to be effective. As formidable as this class of weapons might have been, at any one time the *Luftwaffe* never had more than forty aircrews that were

trained in their use.

The X *Fliegerkorps'* primary problem at the time of D-Day was lack of personnel, not aircraft. For example, as of May 30, 1944, the corps' III *Gruppe* (Group) of *Kampfgeschwader* (Bomber Wing) 100 in Toulouse was equipped with thirty Do-217 bombers but had only seventeen trained crews. Meanwhile, the II *Fliegerkorps*, intended to be the specialized ground-attack force for the Western Front, had virtually no planes available to meet the Allied invasion. Almost all of the *Luftwaffe's* ground-attack aircraft were being thrown into combat against the Soviet summer offensive of 1944. The II *Fliegerkorps* as well as the II *Jagdkorps* were also suffering from a shortage of trained pilots.

In northwestern Europe, the overall disparity between the *Luftwaffe* and USAAF and RAF in June 1944 was staggering. Due to relatively low serviceability rates, of the total of 693 *Luftflotte* 3 aircraft on the ground, Sperrle probably had no more than five hundred ready to fly into battle when the Allies landed. He faced more than seven thousand Allied aircraft flying in support of the invasion.

Although its numbers of aircraft were inadequate to the task, the *Luftwaffe* did possess a very large and very effective flak force stationed along the threatened coast, from Belgium to Brittany. In early 1944, the III Flak Corps had 326 heavy flak batteries of 88mm and 105mm guns and 392 light anti-aircraft batteries of 20mm and 37mm automatic cannons in reserve near the northern French coast, ready to be deployed against an Allied invasion. Since a battery normally had four guns, this force amounted to approximately 2,872 flak guns. Moreover, additional German anti-aircraft forces would be available to repel the invasion. In 1944 each army and SS division included its own flak battalion and sometimes an additional flak battery as well. An army division normally was assigned twelve flak guns, while a *Panzergrenadier* division had up to seventy-four of the guns.

German naval units stationed at all the French and Low Countries ports maintained a considerable number of their own anti-aircraft guns. By 1944 the navy alone had eighty-eight flak battalions, with four to six flak batteries per

Left: Allied bombs pummel Chartres Airfield, southwest of Paris, on June 3, 1944. Ground attacks and bombing raids by the U.S. Army Air Forces before and after D-Day forced the Luftwaffe *to use improvised landing strips and to heavily camouflage its grounded aircraft (below).*

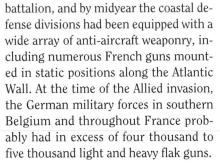

battalion, and by midyear the coastal defense divisions had been equipped with a wide array of anti-aircraft weaponry, including numerous French guns mounted in static positions along the Atlantic Wall. At the time of the Allied invasion, the German military forces in southern Belgium and throughout France probably had in excess of four thousand to five thousand light and heavy flak guns.

Another plus for the *Luftwaffe* was that, in general, its equipment was of excellent quality. The fighter force's Messerschmitt Me-109Gs and Fw-190As were superb aircraft, their primary limitation being a relatively short combat range. The Fw-190's F and G fighter-bomber models attached to the II *Flieger-korps* were among the most effective ground-attack aircraft of the era, and the Ju-88s and Do-217s of *Luftflotte* 3 were excellent light and medium bombers, respectively. Defensively, the III Flak Corps' 88mm heavy guns as well as the rapid-firing 20mm and 37mm light guns, many in multiple mounts, were among the most effective anti-aircraft weapons of World War II.

The *Luftwaffe* was, moreover, supported by an excellent comprehensive radar defense system covering the entire French coast in two belts: a line of Freya radars along the coast itself and another

line of the radars thirty to fifty kilometers inland. In 1944 the Germans had a superb air defense system in the invasion area that featured a radar listening service that intercepted Allied radio and radar transmissions and gave immediate reports to German pilots. Also, German aircraft had an identification friend or foe (IFF) system called the Y-Gerät, by which Würzburg and Freya radars could track German aircraft and direct them to Allied aircraft out to a distance of 250 kilometers.

The only poor-quality *Luftwaffe* equipment the Allies faced was the Heinkel He-177 heavy bomber. It had, on paper, impressive bombload, speed, and flying characteristics, but its engine layout was badly designed. As a result, the bomber suffered from engine fires. Even when the engines did not catch fire, He-177

units had up to a 50 percent aircraft mission abort rate because of overheating.

By the spring of 1944, the German high command knew that the Allied invasion of France was imminent, probably in the Calais area or on Normandy's Cotentin Peninsula. The tempo of the air war was also heating up over Western Europe. As the *Luftwaffe* declined in numbers of aircraft available and capability, the Allied air forces, bolsterd by American productivity, were growing almost daily. Along with their bombing campaign against German industry in the spring of 1944, the RAF and U.S. Eighth and Ninth Air Forces unleashed a massive offensive to cripple the German transportation system throughout France. The ensuing damage to the French railroad network seriously affected *Luftflotte* 3, as transporting parts, fuel, and ammunition to forward airfields became extremely difficult. In addition to the transportation campaign, beginning in May, U.S. bombers hit synthetic fuel plants that produced aviation fuel. The attacks rapidly depleted the *Luftwaffe*'s fuel reserves, already perilously low.

*L*uftflotte 3's weaknesses hampered its implementation of strategies to deal with the invasion threat. The air strategy that Sperrle had proposed in 1943—anti-shipping strikes and long-range reconnaissance over the Atlantic—was strongly supported by the German navy as a means of assisting the U-boat campaign. But such a campaign might have resulted, at best, in a slightly increased level of Allied shipping losses.

The *Luftwaffe*'s most obvious and effective strategy would have been to hold its bomber force in readiness until the Allied fleets and ground forces had assembled in the English ports of embarkation. At that point, German bombing attacks against such highly concentrated Allied targets might have caused considerable damage and disruption to the invasion forces. As it was, only one minor air attack was carried out against the Allied embarkation areas in 1944. On May 30, German night bombers attacked U.S. ordnance units in Falmouth, England, resulting in some casualties. It is doubtful that this attack was part of any deliberate plan.

For such a campaign to succeed, a fairly comprehensive program of aerial reconnaissance would have been required. The *Luftwaffe*, however, flew only a handful of scouting missions over southern England that spring. The few aerial reconnaissance reports that the *Luftwaffe* high command did receive clearly indicated the size and significance of the enemy's naval and troop buildup. For instance, an April 25 reconnaissance mission reported that Southampton and Plymouth were full of landing craft, troop transports, even battleships and cruisers. In Plymouth Harbor on April 28, German airmen spotted three battleships, five cruisers, twenty-four destroyers, and dozens of landing vessels. Finally, what appears to have been the last reconnaissance flight over England prior to the invasion, on May

24, reported that the ports of Bournemouth, Portland, and Weymouth were filled with naval vessels, from battleships to patrol boats to landing craft. Even if the Germans had reacted to such intelligence, it is nevertheless doubtful that more than a handful of bombers could have been deployed against the embarkation ports at this point, and even fewer could have gotten through.

By the spring of 1944, the tempo of the air war was heating up over the Western Front.

The *Luftwaffe* considered an extensive aerial mining operation of the sea approaches to the Pas de Calais and Normandy. The Germans had a superb new naval mine in production in 1944. The pressure, or "Oyster," mine was detonated by changes in hydrostatic pressure caused by a passing ship. Chained to the sea bottom, the mine was extremely difficult to detect and sweep. It would have been fairly simple for the *Luftwaffe* to sow some large minefields in the weeks before D-Day. In this instance, however, the air wing suffered from the well-known "wonder weapon syndrome." Since the mines were new and reflected a major advance in technology, the Germans decided it was too risky to use them before an invasion, in case the Allies should manage to acquire an intact mine and develop countermeasures. The *Luftwaffe* high command accordingly decided that a mining campaign would only be undertaken after the invasion had begun.

One of the primary German operational strategies was to use its large, effective anti-aircraft force to defend the likeliest targets. The *Luftwaffe* also set flak traps, in which obsolete or derelict aircraft were set out on an airfield as decoys and then surrounded by a battery of 20mm and 37mm flak guns. It was hoped that Allied fighter-bombers, attracted by such tempting targets, would take the bait and be shot down in

large numbers.

By early 1944, *Luftflotte* 3 had approximately one hundred airfields within 350 miles of Normandy. Many of these had been bases for the former French and Belgian air forces, with long, hardened runways and good camouflage. The large number of airfields provided *Luftflotte* 3 potential defense in depth as well as flexibility in shifting the short-range fighters around the country. In addition, these planes could be operated from relatively small, grassy fields, camouflaged and hidden among the trees surrounding the fields. *Luftwaffe* groups (thirty to fifty aircraft) were usually based at two or three nearby airfields, which facilitated fairly effective repair and supply support at the squadron and group level and also enhanced airfield defense. It was the norm for two to three heavy and one or two light flak batteries to be assigned to each group of airfields. Because the Germans were unsure when or where the invasion would come, they decided to wait for it and then deploy most of the fighters assigned to German home air defense forward to the many sites in France prepared by *Luftflotte* 3.

When the Allied invasion was finally launched on June 6, the *Luftwaffe* attempted to attack the Allied landings with the very limited forces it had at hand. Yet that day *Luftflotte* 3 flew a mere 319 sorties against the Allies. General Peltz's IX *Fliegerkorps* made the fleet's primary effort, flying 130 bomber sorties against the invasion fleet on the evening of June 6-7. The X *Fliegerkorps* launched forty planes carrying missiles or torpedoes against the Allies on the night of D-Day, but managed to sink not one enemy ship. The *Luftwaffe*'s counteroffensive intensified over the next few days. On June 8, five hundred sorties were flown against the Allied forces off Normandy, but the increased effort yielded few results.

In the days immediately after D-Day, the *Luftwaffe* attempted to wage the kind of air campaign it had conducted against the British and American fleets only a few months before, during the Salerno landings in Italy. Two groups of the X *Fliegerkorps* attacked shipping with Fritz Xs, and other bombers dropped torpedoes. The IX *Fliegerkorps*, with an operational strength of scarcely more than a wing (one hundred bombers), dropped torpedoes and bombs. At Salerno the *Luftwaffe* had been able to inflict considerable damage on Allied shipping during night attacks. German glide bombs disabled the battleship HMS *Warspite* and the cruiser HMS *Uganda* and severely damaged the cruiser USS *Savannah*. In addition, an Allied hospital ship, two merchant vessels, and twenty other craft were sunk off Salerno, most by glide bombs. During the two weeks after D-Day, however, the radio-controlled bombs sank only two Allied vessels and damaged seven; torpedoes sank three ships and damaged two. In contrast to Salerno, where large enemy ships had been disabled, the largest Allied vessel lost from air attack in the waters off Normandy was a destroyer.

Why was the *Luftwaffe*'s campaign against the Allies largely ineffective? First, Allied air superiority over the Normandy front was enormous. On D-Day alone, the Allies flew 14,674 sorties. Also, Allied countermeasures against the *Luftwaffe* in the spring and summer of 1944 had been very effective. The Germans' excellent radar system and communications net had been pounded mercilessly throughout May and June. *Luftwaffe* bomber crews, which had far less training than their Allied counterparts, were highly dependent on good radar control and guidance from ground controllers, but by June 6 no more than 18 percent of the German radar system is estimated to have still been operational. In case the *Luftwaffe* managed to get its radars working and use its communications effectively, the RAF had an entire group of bombers ready to conduct electronic warfare.

Indeed, modern airborne electronic warfare had reached a considerable degree of maturity by D-Day. On the night of June 5, 110 specially equipped RAF bombers belonging to Nos. 1 and 100 Groups patrolled the night-fighter approaches and the invasion area. Transmitter-equipped Avro Lancasters of No. 101 Squadron flew with German-speaking airmen, who attempted to jam enemy communications with their own phony voice transmissions. A radio countermeasures unit with aircraft equipped for radar jamming and deception flew thirty-four sorties on the night of D-Day, and Allied jamming and deception sorties continued on a regular basis throughout June.

Several RAF and USAAF night-fighter squadrons, as well as a vast number of

> **During the Normandy air campaign, British and U.S. anti-aircraft guns probably accounted for more Allied planes shot down than did the Luftwaffe.**

naval anti-aircraft guns, protected the Allied forces. On D-Day itself, the U.S. Ninth Air Force's IX Air Defense Command, a two-brigade-strong anti-aircraft unit, started moving ashore. A very large number of anti-aircraft guns available for forward defense of the beachhead against *Luftwaffe* attacks proved, however, to be a mixed blessing for the Allies. While the vast volume of American and British anti-aircraft fire was often successful in throwing the inadequately trained *Luftwaffe* bomber pilots off their aim, the gunners of the Royal Navy, U.S. Navy, and U.S. Army also had a disturbing tendency to shoot at anything that flew. Though no exact figures are available, there were numerous friendly-fire incidents over Normandy in which Allied anti-aircraft gunners fired on RAF and USAAF planes. Indeed, during the Normandy air campaign, British and U.S. anti-aircraft guns probably accounted for more Allied planes shot down than did the *Luftwaffe*.

One of the most crippling factors affecting the *Luftwaffe*'s conduct of the air campaign was its lack of effective tactical intelligence. The handful of reconnaissance aircraft available to *Luftflotte* 3 was able to provide only the most perfunctory information concerning Allied dispositions. In the absence of clear information on the enemy's fleet and ground troops, German bomber and fighter-bomber units were ordered to attack the beachhead in the hope that, with luck, they might hit something. German intelligence failed in other ways as well. For example, on the night of June 6, German E-boats of the 4th Motor Torpedo Boat Flotilla were ordered to conduct torpedo attacks against the Allied fleet. German intelligence was, however, unable to provide requested information on the draft of the Allied vessels to be attacked. Consequently, the German navy had to arm its torpedoes with contact fuzes rather than more effective magnetic fuzes, which could only be used at preset depths. That lack of basic information about Allied naval forces may offer an additional explanation of why the many torpedoes dropped by *Luftflotte* 3 found so few targets.

As soon as the Allied landings began in Normandy, the *Luftwaffe* began the long-planned shift of most of its home defense forces to airfields near the invasion area—code-named Operation Doktor Gustav. During the first days of the invasion, thirty-one fighter units, including seven hundred to eight hundred aircraft, flew from Germany to France, leaving the Reich air defense with only eight night-fighter groups and three replacement fighter groups—all of limited effectiveness. The X *Fliegerkorps* was also reinforced with forty-five Ju-88 torpedo bombers, and the IX *Fliegerkorps* received an additional ninety bombers. Half the fighters deployed to France were allocated to the II *Fliegerkorps* for ground-attack missions. Although the Fw-190 was a superb ground-attack aircraft, all the pilots deployed from the Reich were trained (minimally) as interceptor pilots; none had received any training in ground attack.

The reinforcement of *Luftflotte* 3 began to unravel almost as soon as it had begun. Because most of the airfields within 150 miles of the Normandy front had been severely battered, the majority of the reinforcing aircraft were diverted to airfields around Paris and in central

France, which were in better shape and more secure but were relatively far from the battlefront. The Allies, on the other hand, were able to build airfields in Normandy immediately upon coming ashore, so that by July a large number of their aircraft were operating from bases only minutes behind the front, maximizing sortie rates and multiplying the effectiveness of the British and U.S. fighter and fighter-bomber force.

Another difficulty faced by the *Luftwaffe* in France was its own deplorable signals security. It preferred to use Enigma cipher machines, even when secure land lines were available, and the *Luftwaffe* had the *Wehrmacht*'s least secure radio code. As a result, for most of the war the German air force was the Allies' best source of signals intelligence. Its unit deployment orders were quickly intercepted and decoded, resulting in RAF and USAAF fighters intercepting and decimating many of the German air units headed to France.

While the *Luftwaffe* was managing to fly five hundred or more sorties a day by June 9, German fighter aircraft, lacking radar because of the Allied pre-invasion air campaign, had little effective ground control. Due to the lack of aerial reconnaissance, the *Luftwaffe*'s fighters, as well as its bombers, had to resort to flying sweeps in the general direction of the beachheads. Allied fighters regularly intercepted such flights, inflicting heavy losses. American and British fighters also regularly intercepted *Luftwaffe* ground-attack aircraft, forcing the German planes to drop their bombs prematurely and abort their missions. Allied air superiority was so overwhelming and the ground-attack missions of the *Luftwaffe* so ineffectual that on June 12 the II *Fliegerkorps* ceased conducting such operations and all of its remaining Fw-190s reverted to a pure interceptor role.

The IX and X *Fliegerkorps*' valiant effort to drop torpedoes and glide bombs on the Allied fleet yielded so few results that after the same date the German bomber force was relegated to less risky mine-laying missions. By August the *Luftwaffe* had sown more than four thousand mines along the sea approaches off Normandy. *Luftflotte* 3's mining campaign of June-July was far more successful than its bombing attacks. Almost nightly the shipping channels and anchorage areas off the Normandy beachhead were mined with airdropped Oyster mines. By July 6, more than six hundred

One of the few bright spots for the Luftwaffe *during the run-up to D-Day and during the Normandy campaign was the performance of its flak units. Above far left: The crew of a camouflaged Flakpanzer IV Wirbelwind (Whirlwind), which was equipped with four 20mm cannons, searches for enemy aircraft. Above left: A Royal Air Force pilot poses next to the flak-damaged tail of his Hawker Typhoon fighter. Left: Gunners prepare their 37mm Flak 18 for action.*

Luftwaffe *"wonder weapons"* that generally proved a bust during the Normandy campaign included the Messerschmitt Me-262 jet (top); the Fritz X radio-guided bomb (inset); and the Mistel (above), an unmanned Ju-88 bomber—fitted with an eighty-four-hundred-pound warhead—that was released from an Fw-190 (shown) or Messerschmitt Me-109 fighter.

a monthly attrition rate of 10-15 percent—virtually all casualties from flak. By June and July, medical officers were commenting on the relatively large number of psychological casualties among the Ninth's surviving aircrews caused by the extreme intensity of the bomber operations and by the stress of constantly flying through highly lethal bursts of flak.

During June, the month of maximum effort by both the German and American air forces, the RAF and USAAF lost 1,564 aircraft over France and Germany, the majority shot down by anti-aircraft fire. The heavy attrition rate imposed by the German flak forces in the spring and in June finally led to a reduction of Allied air activity by July and August. Attrition was heavier than expected, and the air units that had borne the brunt of the pre-invasion air campaign needed a rest. By July the British and Americans had reduced air sorties over France by 20-25 percent. The Ninth Air Force reduced its daily bomber sortie rate from the May-June rate of four hundred sorties to 270 in July. In June the Ninth had flown one thousand fighter-bomber sorties per day, but by July the rate was down to 750.

It is difficult to discuss *Luftwaffe* operations in 1944 without some mention of the "wonder weapons" employed by the Germans, several of them against the Allied forces in Normandy. The Mistel, an obsolete Junkers Ju-88 bomber armed with an eighty-four-hundred-pound warhead and equipped to fly by remote control, was one such weapon. The crewless Junkers was mated with a manned fighter, which was attached above it. The fighter pilot flew both aircraft off the ground and, upon reaching attack altitude and position, released the Ju-88 and guided it into an Allied warship using a simple joystick remote-control device. Theoretically, the Mistel should have been quite lethal, but in actuality the system worked poorly. The weapon was slow, not very maneuverable, and not effective

of the devices had been dropped, and between June 22 and 29 alone, they sank five warships and four other ships off the British beaches. In the American Utah Beach sector, four destroyers and two minesweepers were sunk and twenty-five other vessels damaged during the first ten days of the mining campaign. The mere presence of Oyster mines considerably hampered Allied shipping operations, as vessels could not safely travel faster than four or five knots in areas where mines had been sown or where mining was suspected.

In summary, the *Luftwaffe* made a major effort against the Allies in June 1944. More than one thousand aircraft flew from the Reich to reinforce *Luftflotte* 3. The planes, however, were quickly lost with little to show for the effort. Between June 6 and 30, the *Luftwaffe* flew 13,829 sorties and lost a total of 1,181 aircraft, making June the Ger-

man air force's bloodiest month of 1944.

In contrast to its air operations, Germany's ground-based flak operations in northwestern Europe in the spring and summer of 1944 inflicted heavy RAF and USAAF losses. Prior to the invasion, the *Luftwaffe* was well aware of Allied air targeting strategies and placed heavy flak defenses around the obvious targets, including major transportation nodes—such as vital bridges and rail yards—major airfields, and military command centers. All *Luftwaffe* airfield units and ground operations units were equipped with extra flak guns. According to the U.S. Ninth Air Force's records of the Normandy air campaign, American medium-bomber forces rarely saw German fighter aircraft, but flak was extremely heavy and caused constant heavy attrition of aircraft and aircrews. Between April and July 1944, the medium bombers of the Ninth Air Force had in a high-threat environment.

The *Luftwaffe* nevertheless conducted a number of Mistel sorties against Allied shipping in June and July. The first was typical of the program's performance. On June 24 a flight of five Mistels guided by pilots of the IV *Gruppe* of *Kampfgeschwader* (KG) 101 on its way to attack Allied ships was intercepted by Allied night fighters long before it reached effective range. The Ju-88s were released early, and the mission was aborted.

Another wonder weapon upon which the Germans placed considerable hope was the Messerschmitt Me-262 jet fighter. By D-Day the aircraft had just come into mass production, but the *Luftwaffe* had very few pilots who were even minimally qualified to fly the jet. With higher takeoff and landing speeds than other planes, the Me-262 needed much longer runways and there were also difficulties deploying the planes in France. The short range of the Me-262 meant that it had to operate from forward airfields, but by June the Allied air forces were regularly pounding all of the improved runways in northern France and the Low Countries.

Despite these problems, nine Me-262A-2a fighter-bombers of KG 51 were ordered deployed to France on July 20, 1944—even though the unit rated only four pilots as even moderately competent in the aircraft. A few jets of this unit did take to the skies over France but seem to have made little impression on the Allies. As the average lifespan of a jet turbine engine at this time was about eight hours, repair and logistics posed a major problem for jet operations. With its airfields under constant attack, the Me-262 unit changed bases constantly. That left its mechanics and motor convoys of spare engines and parts attempting to drive all over France trying to keep up with their unit—all the while being bombed and strafed by Allied fighter-bombers. After one month of operations in France, the Me-262s were evacuated to Belgium and then to Germany, but not before one of the ground support convoys of KG 51 became lost, took a wrong turn, and was captured by Allied forces, thence delivering a new jet turbine engine to the Allies.

The *Luftwaffe*'s operations against the Allied landings at Normandy are an important example of a technologically advanced but outnumbered air force waging a defensive campaign against an enemy with equal technology but far greater aircraft and trained pilot resources. There was no chance at all that the *Luftwaffe* could have held on to air superiority over France in 1944 the way it had against the RAF air offensives of 1941-42. The combined industrial production of the United States and British Commonwealth ensured that the Allies would have an enormous aircraft numerical superiority. Moreover, the *Luftwaffe*'s most serious deficiency was its small supply of trained pilots—and the

> **The Germans placed considerable hope in the *Me-262*, but the *Luftwaffe* had very few pilots who were even minimally qualified to fly the jet.**

Germans had lost that race when the pilot training programs were reduced in late 1942.

Germany, however, had several strategic and operational options that could have ensured a much more effective role for the *Luftwaffe* in the Normandy campaign. At the strategic level, Hitler and Göring's decision to waste the carefully built-up bomber fleet in terror attacks on English population centers has to rank as one of history's worst misuses of air power. Had the IX *Fliegerkorps* been held in reserve for use against Allied sea and troop concentrations before D-Day, it might have caused considerable losses and disruption to the Allied forces.

Considering the effectiveness of the Oyster mines once they were used, the operational decision to use extensive aerial mining only after the Allied landings also was a poor one. In addition, the *Luftwaffe* was very badly served by its intelligence system, which provided little useful information about pre–D-Day Allied ground and naval forces, and by the high command's refusal to build up a reserve of bomber aircrews well trained in the use of radio-controlled glide bombs. Using Fritz Xs and given good targeting information, crews could still not have stopped the Allied landings, but they likely would have produced considerable Allied casualties.

On the other hand, the *Luftwaffe*'s flak forces were extremely effective in 1944 and demonstrated that they could influence an air campaign by inflicting heavy casualties and gradually wearing down the British and U.S. air forces. The Allies, for their part, made few strategic or operational mistakes during the Normandy air war. Their targeting of the German radar network and the use of extensive electronic warfare to cripple the enemy defenses was on the whole brilliantly conducted.

The Allied strategy of bombing German oil facilities was sound. As that aerial campaign began, the enemy's stocks of aviation fuel quickly dwindled, and the *Luftwaffe* had no chance to ever recover. British and American defenses over the invasion fleet and beachhead were effective and well planned. Moreover, the Allied engineers enabled the RAF and USAAF fighter and medium-bomber units to quickly relocate to France, where they could maximize their effectiveness while holding the Germans to long-range operations.

The only mistake of the Allied air campaign was to use fighter-bombers in low-level attacks against *Luftwaffe* airfields. This cost the enemy some aircraft and inflicted some casualties, but the heavy price in lost U.S. and British aircraft and pilots was not worth it. Heavy-bomber raids on German airfields were less accurate but did the trick in disrupting *Luftwaffe* logistics and forcing the Germans to use airfields out of effective range of the beachhead.

JAMES S. CORUM is the author of *The Luftwaffe: Creating the Operational Air War, 1918-1940* (University Press of Kansas, 1997) and co-author of *Airpower in Small Wars: Fighting Insurgents and Terrorists* (University Press of Kansas, 2003).

SCREAMING EAGLES
in Normandy

In their baptism of fire, the green paratroopers of General Maxwell Taylor's 101st Airborne Division performed like seasoned veterans.

by **JOHN M. TAYLOR**

The darkened skies over Normandy are filled with the parachutes of American airborne soldiers in the early morning hours of June 6, 1944. The D-Day drop was the first combat mission for the 101st and the "rendezvous with destiny" that the "Screaming Eagles" had been promised by the division's founder, Maj. Gen. William C. Lee, when the unit was activated on August 16, 1942 (R.G. Smith, courtesy of Sharlyn Marsh).

At approximately 1:30 A.M. on June 6, 1944, the commander of the 101st Airborne Division landed heavily in a French pasture near the village of Ste. Marie-du-Mont in Normandy. Major General Maxwell Taylor had no time to reflect on the fact that he was the first United States general ever to parachute into combat, as well as the first American general on enemy soil in Operation Overlord, the Allied invasion of France.

Manipulating his shroud lines, Taylor narrowly avoided a tree. Next he struggled to extricate himself from his harness. From a nearby field came the sound of a German machine pistol like "a ripping seat of pants." After ten frustrating minutes of fighting buckles and snaps, Taylor used a knife to cut himself free. Pistol in one hand and an identifying metal "cricket" in the other, the general set out in the darkness in search of American soldiers.

The 101st was one of three Allied airborne divisions supporting the amphibious assault on Normandy. The British 6th Airborne Division had the task of securing bridges on the eastern flank of the landing beaches. The U.S. 82nd Division had as its primary missions the sealing of the central Cotentin Peninsula from any attack from the south and the destruction of bridges over the Douve River north of its junction with the Merderet. The 101st was to secure the exits of four causeways behind Utah Beach, Exits 1, 2, 3, and 4; destroy bridges over the Douve northwest of Carentan; and capture two bridges northeast of the town.

These were ambitious objectives, particularly because a few weeks earlier the role, if any, to be played by the Allied airborne had been very much in question. Although airborne advocates such as Generals Matthew B. Ridgway, James M. Gavin, and Taylor were sold on the concept of "vertical envelopment," the Allied high command was not. In Sicily, elements of the 82nd had been dropped so haphazardly that some paratroopers drowned in the Mediterranean. In addition, despite an elaborate system of recognition signals, aircraft carrying American paratroopers from North Africa to Sicily had been shot down by trigger-happy gunners on U.S. Navy vessels.

Major General Maxwell Taylor, a veteran of the 82nd Airborne Division, did not have long to become acquainted with the men of the 101st prior to the invasion. He assumed command of the division on March 14, 1944, after Lee had suffered a heart attack and been relieved.

In the weeks leading up to Overlord, Air Marshal Trafford Leigh-Mallory, General Dwight D. Eisenhower's deputy for air, had predicted disaster for the airborne operations. German fighters and flak, he believed, would inflict severe losses on the slow-moving C-47 transports. Moreover, while some soldiers could be evacuated from the beaches if Overlord should fail, paratroopers dropped farther inland would be at the mercy of German defenders. Leigh-Mallory was even more caustic with regard to the proposed glider landings, predicting that casualties "will not only prove fatal to success of the operation itself but will…jeopardize all future airborne operations." Nevertheless, Lt. Gen. Omar Bradley insisted that the airborne assault was essential to the success of Overlord, and Supreme Allied Commander Eisenhower supported him.

If gliders were to be used, Leigh-Mallory wanted operations to begin at dusk on June 6 rather than in the predawn. Ridgway, however, argued successfully that the lightly armed airborne troops would require their pack artillery and communications from the outset on D-Day. Ridgway carried his point, but

the glider operation remained a challenge. Tall poles erected in possible landing areas—"Rommel asparagus"—were one problem; the Norman hedgerows were another. A typical hedgerow, designed to control cattle, began with a stone wall about three feet high. Soil was then packed around the wall, and shrubs and trees planted on top. For the Germans, every hedgerow was a natural defensive barrier; for an incoming glider, every hedgerow was a potential deathtrap.

And the Germans were ready. Five divisions, plus several smaller units, were stationed in the area of the Allied landings. One of these was the 91st Air Landing Division, which had been en route to Brittany when diverted to the Cotentin Peninsula. Another potent reinforcement was the thirty-five-hundred-man 6th *Fallschirmjäger* (Paratroop) Regiment.

The 101st's role called for its parachute component, sixty-six hundred men in three regiments, to land in darkness and secure the four causeways leading inland from Utah Beach. It was a vital assignment, for the Germans had flooded low-lying areas behind the beaches, obliging any invading force to funnel across a few causeways in order to move inland. Overlord would be primarily a parachute operation for the 101st, because the one area where Leigh-Mallory carried the day concerned the gliders. Since they would come in after the Germans had been alerted by paratroop landings, the division was allocated only fifty-two gliders, enough for about three hundred men and some pack artillery. Most of the division's 327th Glider Infantry Regiment became part of the amphibious landing.

Army airborne divisions were elite units, and paratroopers were volunteers. Most officers were in their twenties, and many enlisted men were no more than seventeen or eighteen. But the 101st Division, unlike the 82nd, was as yet unbloodied. The practice in World War I had been to allow a new division to get its bearings in a quiet sector before moving into the front lines. There would be no quiet sector for Taylor's "Screaming Eagles." They would drop into German-occupied Normandy, where training and zeal would have to compensate for lack of combat experience.

If the 101st was an elite unit, the

Troop Carrier Command (TCC) was not. The air corps' best pilots opted for fighters and bombers; the transports got what was left. Moreover, TCC pilots had not been trained in night flying or in formation flying in bad weather. As Stephen Ambrose has noted, "The possibility of a midair collision was on every pilot's mind." During the first hours of D-Day, when the great armada of C-47s encountered both clouds and groundfire, formation flying went by the board and many paratroopers were dropped wherever it seemed most convenient.

For a variety of reasons, the American paratroopers underwent a wild night. In the words of one survivor, men landed "in pastures, plowed fields, grain fields, orchards, and hedgerows. They landed at the base of antiglider poles, in tall trees and small trees. They landed on rooftops, in cemeteries, town squares, backyards, paved roads, and in roadside ditches. They landed in canals, rivers, bogs, and flooded areas."

Private John Fitzgerald jumped, looked up to check his parachute, and watched as enemy bullets ripped through it. "I was mesmerized by the scene," he later recalled, adding that

Every color of the rainbow was flashing through the sky. Equipment bundles attached to chutes that did not fully open came hurtling past me, helmets that had been ripped off by the opening shock, troopers floated past. Below me, figures were running in all directions....My chute floated into the branches of an apple tree and dumped me to the ground with a thud.

Not everyone was so fortunate as Fitzgerald. More than one entire stick, or planeload, of paratroopers was dropped into the Channel and drowned. Private Donald Burgett watched from the ground as one C-47 came in low across the field where he had just landed. The parachutes were just starting to open as the troopers hit the ground. Burgett thought they made a sound like ripe pumpkins being thrown down and bursting. Some luckier ones were dropped on Utah Beach itself, or in water shallow enough to permit them to discard heavy equipment and make their way to land. Still others landed in marshes that had been flooded by the Germans and barely avoided the fate of

Above: Dead glidermen lie in a Norman field beside the wreck of their British-made Horsa. By all accounts, landing in a glider was a terrifying and dangerous experience. The 101st's assistant division commander, Brig. Gen. Donald F. Pratt, was killed when his glider landed in Normandy and crashed into a tree. Right: Floyd Talbert (front) and Campbell Smith, members of Company E, 506th Parachute Infantry Regiment, pass the body of a German paratrooper as they move along a Norman hedgerow.

those dropped in the Channel.

At dawn, of the sixty-six hundred paratroopers of the 101st, perhaps one thousand were at or near division objectives. Others were as far as ten miles away. The glider operation proved far more precise than the parachute drop, with forty-nine out of fifty-two gliders reaching their landing zones. But glider landings were hardly landings at all. No glider that went into Normandy ever saw service again, and some were so thoroughly destroyed that soldiers had difficulty removing the cargo. Taylor's assistant division commander, Brig. Gen. Donald F. Pratt, went in by glider and became the first American general to die in Normandy. "We slid over 800 feet on wet grass and smashed into trees at 50 miles per hour," his pilot recalled. Pratt was crushed by his glider's cargo and died of a broken neck.

FORREST GUTH VIA JOHN POWERS

With pistol in hand, Taylor had initially made his way along a hedgerow in what he supposed to be the direction of others in his stick. After about twenty minutes he detected movement along one hedgerow. When he heard the click of a cricket he responded with a double-click. "There in the dim moonlight was the first American soldier to greet me," Taylor would recall, "a sight of martial beauty." The two embraced silently, then moved off in search of others.

It took the remainder of the short

Paratroopers gather around the water pump at Ste. Marie-du-Mont on the afternoon of June 6 to talk with local French civilians. The distinct onion shape of the village's church steeple served as an important reference point for men of the 101st as they attempted to get their bearings and organize themselves after landing in Normandy.

summer night for Taylor to assemble a few dozen soldiers, most of them assigned to division headquarters. He gathered his officers in a clearing, where they decided to stay put until they could get their bearings. By daylight, Taylor had with him perhaps ninety men, including Chief of Staff Colonel Jerry Higgins, artillery commander Brig. Gen. Tony McAuliffe, division engineer Lt. Col. John Pappas, and Lt. Col. Julian Ewell, a battalion commander in the 501st Regiment. The group was so short of riflemen that Taylor was heard to remark, "Never before have so few been commanded by so many." But the dawn's first rays revealed the distinctive onion-shaped steeple of the Ste. Marie-du-Mont church nearby, and the Americans knew where they were.

Scattered across the Cotentin Peninsula, American paratroopers implemented a directive laid down in training: If a unit did not reach its drop zone, it should carry out those missions assigned to the area where it found itself. The headquarters group was close to its drop zone and did not have to implement a fallback plan. Taylor sent several officers off to establish a division headquarters at the village of Hiesville, while he and the remainder of his band set out toward Utah Beach.

The men of the 101st had had little time to get to know their commanding general. Forty-three years old and a graduate of West Point, Taylor was given command of the division in March after his predecessor, Maj. Gen. William C. Lee, had suffered a heart attack. There was nothing avuncular about Taylor, and he did not inspire universal affection. When he spoke to one of his men, he addressed him crisply as "soldier." But there was something about Taylor that suggested confidence and compe-

An airborne captain gets directions from Norman farmers. The drops scattered American paratroopers all over the Cotentin Peninsula and forced many of them to rely on assistance from local civilians.

tence. In England he had told his men: "All paratroopers are hell-raisers. During the first 24 hours after you jump, raise all the hell you can."

There were many small clashes in the early hours of June 6, but the initial German reaction to the airborne landings was confusion and uncertainty. In the words of historian David Howarth, "The Americans knew what was happening, but few of them knew where they were; the Germans knew where they were, but none of them knew what was happening." Reports of paratrooper landings poured into German headquarters, but no pattern was discernable.

Captain Ernst During commanded a German machine gun company at Brevands, near where the Vire River empties into the Channel. He had been asleep for a couple of hours when, shortly after midnight on the night of June 5-6, he was awakened by the sound of explosions:

There was the noise of many planes coming from the direction of Ste. Mère-Eglise. I thought to myself, This is it! I got dressed as quickly as I could....

When I got to my command post I telephoned battalion headquarters two miles to the rear and said, "Paratroops have landed here." The answer came back, "Here, too," then the line went dead....

Then I heard strange sounds—a kind of "click, click, click" at regular intervals. It sounded like the castanets of Spanish dancers. I couldn't explain it....I felt very uneasy and isolated.

Elsewhere, a German patrol mistook Taylor's jumpmaster, Major Larry Legere, and a companion for French farmers. Challenged by the Germans, Legere explained in French that they were returning from a visit to his cousin. As he spoke, he pulled the pin of a grenade, which exploded among the unsuspecting Germans.

Prisoners were an encumbrance for small groups of paratroopers, and those taken were expected to be totally docile. When one group of prisoners attempted to jump their captors, Sergeant Bill Guarnere shot each in turn with his pistol. "No remorse," he recalled many years later. "No pity. It was as easy as stepping on a bug."

After a hike of about four miles, Taylor's group made its first real contact

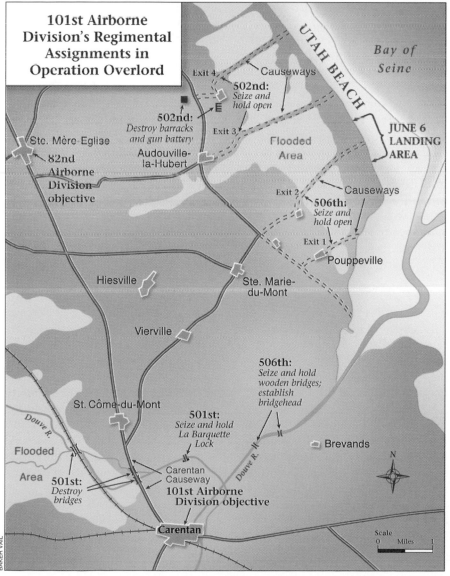

101st Airborne Division's Regimental Assignments in Operation Overlord

UTAH BEACH

Bay of Seine

Exit 4

Causeways

502nd:
Seize and hold open

502nd:
Destroy barracks and gun battery

Exit 3

Ste. Mère-Eglise

82nd Airborne Division objective

Audouville-la-Hubert

Flooded Area

JUNE 6 LANDING AREA

Exit 2

Causeways

506th:
Seize and hold open

Exit 1

Pouppeville

Hiesville

Ste. Marie-du-Mont

Vierville

506th:
Seize and hold wooden bridges; establish bridgehead

St. Côme-du-Mont

Brevands

Douve R.

501st:
Seize and hold La Barquette Lock

Flooded Area

501st:
Destroy bridges

Carentan Causeway

101st Airborne Division objective

Douve R.

N

Carentan

Scale
0 Miles 1

Above: Members of the 101st assemble German prisoners taken shortly after landing. The Germans in and around the 101st's landing area were a mixed lot. While some, as pictured here, were old men or even foreign "volunteers," others, such as the 6th Fallschirmjäger Regiment, were among the best troops Adolf Hitler had available.

with the enemy at about 9 A.M. near Pouppeville, at the base of the southern-most causeway leading to Utah Beach. The German garrison put up stiff resistance from inside the stone houses of the village, and Taylor nearly became a casualty when a badly aimed grenade from one of his soldiers bounced off a house and exploded among the paratroopers. By noon, however, the Americans had occupied the village, killing or wounding thirty Germans and taking forty prisoners at the cost of twenty U.S. casualties.

One of Taylor's aides saw troops moving to the east and fired an identification flare. The newcomers were an advance party from the U.S. 4th Division, and they were able to tell the paratroopers that the landings at Utah Beach were going smoothly. Word also arrived that troopers from the 101st had reached the remaining causeways from the beach.

To the north, causeway Exits 3 and 4 had been the objectives of the 502nd Regiment, led by acting commander Lt. Col. John "Mike" Michaelis. He and his three battalion commanders gathered what men they could find and headed toward their objectives. Lieutenant Colonel Robert G. Cole's battalion captured the unguarded Exit 3 without a fight before moving north to where Michaelis was encountering considerable resistance.

Near Exit 4, Colonel Pat Cassidy, commanding a battalion of the 502nd, had ordered one of his noncoms, Sergeant Harrison Summers, to assemble some men and clear out a nearby barracks complex, code-named X,Y,Z. Summers knew none of the men in his impromptu squad, and as they neared the stone farm buildings serving as barracks, Summers set out on his own. Armed with a submachine gun, he kicked open the door of the first building, ducked inside, and opened fire, killing four German soldiers. He was joined there by a captain from the 82nd, but as the two moved toward a second building the captain fell dead. Summers, alone, slipped into the building, where he gunned down six more Germans.

Summers' squad had largely been spectators thus far, but now Private John Camien joined the sergeant. The two went through five more buildings, killing thirty more enemy soldiers. The final building in the complex turned out to be the mess hall. Bursting through the door, the amazed Americans found fifteen Germans still at breakfast and shot them all. By this time Summers and Camien had the support of a bazooka team, and some fifty Germans still in the complex chose to run for it. Many were cut down, while others were taken prisoner.

A second important clash took place near Exit 2, where the Germans had a battery of 105mm cannons dug into hedgerows overlooking Utah Beach. Captain Richard Winters of the 506th was given a dozen men and directed to take care of the battery.

Winters went to work, telling his makeshift command to discard all their equipment except weapons and ammunition. He explained that their attack would be supported by flanking fire—two machine guns as close to the enemy as possible. Winters' force brought the enemy guns under fire from three sides, one by one. In turn, the Germans with-

drew. One of the attacking Americans, Sergeant Carwood Lipton, recalled: "We fought as a team without standout stars....We didn't have anyone who leaped up and charged a machine-gun. We knocked it out or made it withdraw by maneuver and teamwork or mortar fire."

Historian Max Hastings has noted that "all wars become a matter of small private battles to those who are fighting them." This was notably true in the struggle for Normandy, where one could rarely see more than one hundred to two hundred yards in any direction, and where infantry was often out of touch with armor. The attrition within infantry units was high, and nowhere higher than in the airborne divisions, which had yet to locate their glider-borne artillery. It took the 101st three days to collect scattered paratroopers, acquire some vehicles, and clear out areas of resistance north of the Douve River.

There was a lot to learn. Although the Americans had been briefed about hedgerows, they were not prepared for their size. A trooper from the 82nd, Sergeant Fred Schlemmer, recalled, "We assumed that they would be similar to the English hedgerows, which were like small fences that the fox hunters jumped over." Instead, the invaders were confronted with great banks of foliage that made every road a potential revetment ideal for defense.

As evening turned into night, Taylor made his way to the division headquarters at Hiesville, satisfied that the landings at Utah Beach were proceeding well but ignorant of the situation elsewhere because his radios were still missing. In quickly securing the invasion causeways, the 101st had made a major contribution to the success of Overlord. In a second mission, however—destruction of the Douve River bridges—his men had run into difficulties. The unit responsible, Colonel Howard R. "Jumpy" Johnson's 501st Regiment, had been badly scattered and subsequently encountered severe resistance. Johnson gained a toehold on the river at the La Barquette locks but could not reach the bridges.

Elsewhere the record was also mixed. The British glider forces had found their

landing zones and quickly captured bridges over the Orne River. Ridgway's 82nd Division, however, had had a dreadful drop; not only were its paratroopers scattered but fewer than half of its gliders had reached their designated landing areas. A force from the 82nd, aided by some men of the 101st, captured Ste. Mère-Eglise shortly after dawn on D-Day, but was subjected to fierce enemy counterattacks for the remainder of the day.

As darkness fell on D-Day, the extent of the Allied foothold was less than Eisenhower had hoped. Instead of controlling beachheads six miles deep, as the high command had projected, Allied forces were no more than five miles inland anywhere, and their hold in several areas was precarious. In contrast to the relative ease with which Utah Beach had been secured, the landings on Omaha Beach had been extremely costly; the U.S. 1st and 29th Divisions clung to an enclave less than a mile deep. Bodies, wrecked landing craft, and detritus of war littered the area where twenty-five hundred Americans had died.

Carentan, with about four thousand residents, was the most important population center in the American sector of Normandy. Located on the main highway from Caen to Cherbourg, it was a stop on the Paris–Cherbourg train line as well. More immediate, it was the designated place where Lt. Gen. J. Lawton Collins' VII Corps from Utah Beach was to link up with the V Corps from Omaha Beach. The commander of the 6th *Fallschirmjäger* Regiment, Lt. Col. Friedrich A. von der Heydte, had been instructed by Field Marshal Erwin Rommel to defend the town to the last man.

By the evening of June 7, Taylor had decided that he must seize St. Côme-du-Mont on the Carentan–Cherbourg road before proceeding against Carentan itself. As long as enemy forces held St. Côme-du-Mont they could threaten the advance from Utah Beach, while capture of the village would eliminate this threat and remove the last important point of resistance north of the Douve.

Taylor ordered the 506th's Colonel Robert F. Sink, one of his most aggressive regimental commanders, to attack St. Côme-du-Mont on the morning of June 8. Sink gathered nearly four battalions from various units and attacked at daybreak. The morning saw sharp fighting and repeated German counterattacks. By early afternoon, however, the village was in U.S. hands and the surviving Germans had retreated across the Douve. Taylor told Collins that the river had been secured. "All right," the VII Corps commander replied, "Now take Carentan."

Bradley and Collins were eager to maintain some momentum to compensate for the slow buildup on the beaches. The Allied enclaves remained vulnerable, especially to armor, and might have been in serious jeopardy had Adolf Hitler committed his panzer reserves and released the Fifteenth Army from around Calais, where it served as a hedge against a second Allied landing. Fortunately for the Allies, the Germans were showing the effects of incessant air attacks during the buildup to D-Day. So uncertain was the prospect of division-level reinforcement that local commanders were compelled to feed small units into gaps in the line.

That same day, Taylor met with his senior commanders and outlined a plan for attacking Carentan from three sides. The 327th was to cross the Douve near Brevands and clear the area north of the town, while Colonel Sink's 506th was to move to the west around Carentan and seize a rise known as Hill 30. Meanwhile, the 502nd would advance south along the main highway.

If Taylor had any favorite among his four regiments it was the hard-fighting 506th, with whom he had spent much of D-Day. He also had confidence in the 502nd, even though it had a new commanding officer. Colonel George Moseley, its colorful commander, had broken his leg in landing and was being trundled about in a wheelbarrow when Taylor found him. Taylor ordered the colonel to an aid station and turned over command of the 502nd to Colonel Mike Michaelis.

The advance on Carentan was begun by the 502nd on the morning of June 10. Progress was slow because of German resistance and continuing problems posed by flooded marshlands. Later that morning, the 327th crossed the Douve but soon bogged down. Taylor had har-

U.S. ARMY

After helping the 4th Infantry Division advance inland from Utah Beach, Taylor's men set out to seize strategically vital Carentan (left). When the advance of his 3rd Battalion, 502nd Parachute Infantry Regiment, down the Carentan Causeway (in photo at left, from upper left to Carentan) ran into trouble, Lt. Col. Robert Cole (below left) led a bayonet charge that cleared the enemy. Below center: Major John Stopka assisted in the attack. Below right: After Carentan's capture, Cole poses with 1st Sgt. Hubert Odens (second from left), a Sergeant O'Riley (third from left), and Stopka (right).

PHOTOS: NATIONAL ARCHIVES

Members of one of the 81st Anti-Aircraft Battalion's anti-tank batteries pass GIs from the 101st Division's 327th Glider Infantry Regiment after Carentan's liberation on June 12, 1944. By July 10, when the remnants of the division were finally relieved and began their journey back to England, the 101st had suffered 4,670 casualties. Although it had the second highest total losses of the VII Corps divisions, the 101st had proved itself in combat and, equally important, demonstrated the effectiveness of airborne forces to the Allied high command.

bored reservations about its commander for several days; he now sacked him after a mishandled attack. Calling for Colonel Joseph H. "Bud" Harper, who had been acting as a beachmaster, Taylor gave him command of the glider infantry and briefed him on his role in the move against Carentan. The forty-two-year-old Harper, who had been an agriculture major at the University of Delaware, would lead the glider infantry regiment for the remainder of the war.

The toughest fighting may have been along the exposed St. Côme-du-Mont–Carentan highway, also known as the Carentan Causeway but later referred to by U.S. paratroopers as "Purple Heart Lane." The two-lane road ran straight as an arrow, and the surrounding flooded marshlands made off-road movement difficult.

On the afternoon of June 10, Colonel Cole's 502nd battalion began a cautious advance along the highway toward Carentan. Resistance was stiff, and even included an attack by enemy dive

bombers. Cole's battalion was nearing the town when it came under heavy fire from a nearby farmhouse. Shortly after first light on the eleventh, after ordering smoke from the artillery, Cole led his three companies in one of the few bayonet charges of the war.

At first only about sixty paratroopers followed Cole and his executive officer, Major John Stopka. Then more soldiers sprinted out of the ditches, and the attack gained momentum. The Americans overran the farmhouse and kept going, grenading and bayoneting enemy soldiers in rifle pits and behind hedgerows. Cole, who survived Normandy only to die in Holland, became the first Screaming Eagle to earn the Medal of Honor.

Even as Cole led his charge, the 327th advanced against Carentan from the northeast, moving through a wooded area adjoining a canal. Three companies crossed the canal on the morning of June 11, but were able to advance only a few hundred yards before being halted by heavy fire. That evening, however, the

advance resumed. Sink's 506th pressed toward Hill 30 southeast of Carentan, and Taylor moved Johnson's 501st from a defensive position north of the Douve and threw it into the attack.

By this time fighting had reached the outskirts of Carentan and the town was taking a beating. It was under fire not only from the airborne's artillery but also from massive naval guns offshore and from tank destroyers up from Omaha Beach. In the early hours of June 12, Sink captured Hill 30 and sent a battalion into Carentan itself. The other attackers made their way into the town within hours.

The airborne pincers had achieved their objective, but the Germans slipped away. Colonel von der Heydte pulled out of Carentan on the night of June 11 and set up a new defense line to the southwest. The German commander would be sharply criticized for his withdrawal because the 17th Panzer Division was even then moving to reinforce Carentan, but the Germans were almost out of ammunition, and withdrawal may have been the only prudent course.

Taylor himself was in Carentan on the morning of June 12, eager to continue the attack. But the advance south was sluggish, reflecting the weariness of troops who had been in almost continuous action for six days. In any case, an immediate threat from the enemy ruled out any further advance. At dawn on June 13, tanks from the 17th Panzer appeared and drove the 506th and 501st back to the outskirts of Carentan. Because airborne divisions had few anti-tank weapons, the situation was serious. Taylor would recall that he might have had considerable difficulty "had not General Bradley, unsolicited, sent us the reinforcement of a combat command of the 2nd Armored Division." Bradley was in fact quite concerned for the 101st, because he had Ultra intelligence—decoded German radio messages—indicating that a panzer attack was imminent. Bradley later recalled, "This was one of the few times in the war when I unreservedly believed Ultra and reacted to it tactically."

By midmorning on June 13 an element of the 2nd Armored was in Carentan, and Taylor was conferring with the task force commander, Brig. Gen. Maurice Rose. That afternoon, Sherman tanks equipped with bulldozer blades turned south, with paratroopers deployed on each side. The tanks crashed through hedgerows, driving the German panzers back several miles. The next afternoon, soldiers from Sink's 506th were running routine patrols in Carentan.

The 101st's role in Operation Overlord was almost over. On June 29 the division was withdrawn from Carentan and moved north for occupation duty near Cherbourg. The troops were due some relief. Since D-Day the division had suffered more than forty-six hundred casualties, over one-third of its strength.

For the Allied high command, however, the work of the airborne divisions, on which such care had been lavished, was a source of relief and satisfaction. Despite heavy casualties— and those in the 82nd were even higher than those in the 101st—the airborne component had made a major contribu-

tion to the success of Overlord. Bradley, who had told Eisenhower that he could not order landings at Utah Beach without the airborne operation, was elated. As for Eisenhower, asked many years later what had been his most satisfying moment in the war, he replied that it was when he heard that his two airborne divisions had reached Normandy.

Taylor, in assessing the campaign in his official report, considered both tangibles and intangibles. The most visible benefit had been the 101st's contribution to the almost bloodless landing at

THE AMERICANS OVERRAN THE FARM-HOUSE AND KEPT GOING, GRENADING AND BAYONETING ENEMY SOLDIERS IN RIFLE PITS AND BEHIND HEDGEROWS.

Utah Beach. Less quantifiable was the confusion that the parachute landings had sown in the mind of the enemy. "An airborne landing at night," Taylor wrote, "has a devastating effect on the enemy. It upsets his command organization and prevents the movement of his reserves and artillery." Although the attacker's plans may go awry in the fog of war, "the disruptive effect of the attack on the enemy" more than compensates.

At the same time, Taylor was not inclined toward complacency. He called attention to the heavy losses in equipment delivered by parachute, estimating these to be about 60 percent. The general had harsh words for the Troop Carrier Command, noting that the scattered drop of his division had undone much of the careful training the men had undergone.

Taylor drew a number of conclusions from the Normandy operation. First, an airborne division should not be expected to function as a unit for at least twenty-four hours after landing. In this initial period, any results must come from "the

aggressive action of small groups." Second, airborne units require prompt support from heavier forces. In Taylor's judgment, the pre–D-Day assumption that an airborne division could maintain itself independently for two or three days should be revised downward. Third, the element of surprise inherent in an airborne operation should be exploited to the fullest. For that reason, and to mitigate the absence of heavy weapons, "it may be more economical of lives to land directly on the enemy than to come down at a distance and close with him."

Taylor's final conclusion was rooted in personal experience. "There is an immediate requirement," he wrote, "for a quick release harness." He had not forgotten his ten uncomfortable minutes in that Norman pasture.

The campaign in Normandy was only the first for the Screaming Eagles, who would serve in Holland during the Arnhem campaign and whose legendary defense of Bastogne during the Battle of the Bulge would blunt Hitler's last offensive. The 101st would become the first entire division to be awarded the Distinguished Unit Citation, now called the Presidential Unit Citation.

Decades later, British historian John Keegan reflected on the contribution of the American airborne to the success of D-Day: "Like pioneers in an unknown land, ignorant of its language and landmarks, uncertain of what danger the next thicket or stream-bottom might hold, confident only in themselves and their mastery of the weapons in their hands, the best and bravest of them had stifled their fears, marched forth and planted the roots of settlement in the soil that was there for the taking."

In an impromptu speech at Cherbourg as the 101st prepared to return to Britain, Taylor put the matter more bluntly: "You hit the ground running toward the enemy. You have proved the German soldier is no superman. You have beaten him on his own ground and you can beat him on any ground." And so they would.

JOHN M. TAYLOR is a frequent contributor to *MHQ*. His books include a biography of his famous father, *An American Soldier: The Wars of General Maxwell Taylor* (Presidio Press, 2001).

ANTWERP
Allies' Missed Opportunity

Exploiting the victory in Normandy, British forces seized the strategically located port of Antwerp in early September, but wasted their chance to capture its water approaches and cut off a nearby German army.

by **Alistair Horne**

By the end of August 1944, the Allies had brought the Normandy campaign to a triumphant conclusion, sweeping the Germans back almost to the frontiers of Adolf Hitler's Third Reich. Nevertheless, after this great victory three serious Allied strategic errors marred the closing stages of World War II in Europe and indeed prolonged it—Arnhem, Antwerp, and Ardennes. Although all begin with the letter "A," none deserved better than a D-minus grade, if that. All were interconnected, located in one small corner of the Low Countries. The most fateful of them all, and possibly the most avoidable, was Antwerp—the failure to seize the approaches to the vital Belgian port in early September. For this oversight, all the Allied leaders, from Winston Churchill and Sir Alan Brooke, to Franklin D. Roosevelt and George C. Marshall, to notably Dwight D. Eisenhower and Bernard L. Montgomery, must share the blame.

Of the present day's leading American historians, Carlo D'Este put it in bluntest terms: Antwerp was "one of the great blunders of the war. The importance of a bridgehead across the Rhine notwithstanding, the greatest Allied priority in September 1944 was the capture and opening of Antwerp, one of the world's largest deep-water ports."

Antwerp had been the focus of two great sieges during its long history. A prosperous shipping and banking center during the sixteenth century, the port also became the center of Protestantism in Western Europe, which drew the ire of ultra-Catholic King Philip II—in whose fiefdom it lay—down upon it. Sacked by Philip's Spanish forces in 1576, Antwerp was subjected to a fourteen-month siege led by the duke of Parma in 1584-85.

Napoleon Bonaparte, with his legendary *coup d'oeil*, had realized the strategic value that Antwerp's geography gave it. To comprehend the significance of what was to follow a century and a half later, it is essential to bear in mind the area's extraordinary and complex topography. The vast port itself, in fact, lies up the deep but narrow Scheldt River. It stretches some sixty miles in from the North Sea, of which 34½ miles actually lie in Dutch territory. The mouth of the river's western estuary, the West Scheldt, is in fact commanded by

the Dutch ports of Flushing to the north and Breskens to the south, just three miles apart across the water. To the north, like gills of a fish, there reach out to the sea a series of convoluted promontories and dike-protected islands, wrested painstakingly out of the sea by the patient Dutch and which over the centuries have become peninsulas. Principal of these is Walcheren, on which the port of Flushing lies. By the twentieth century, it was connected to Antwerp and the main body of Holland by the narrow isthmus of South Beveland, only three thousand yards across, with access along a single highway. The isthmus separates the Scheldt's West and East Estuaries. As every would-be exploiter of Antwerp was to discover through the ages, without command of the Scheldt and its approaches, Antwerp was useless.

Bent on an all-out invasion of England in 1803, Napoleon recognized that Antwerp—little more than one hundred miles from England—had all the potential to become as important a naval base as Portsmouth, and he ordered vast sums of money spent to build a dockyard capable of servicing twenty-five large men-of-war. His appreciation was correct, for between Antwerp and Brest in Brittany, far to the west, there was no comparable deep-water port. Boulogne (where Napoleon was congregating most

Supreme Allied Expeditionary Force Commander Dwight D. Eisenhower confers with his controversial subordinate, British Field Marshal Bernard L. Montgomery. Historians are divided over which one deserves chief blame for the lengthy delay in securing the approaches to Antwerp.

NATIONAL ARCHIVES

of his shallow-draft invasion craft), Calais, Dunkirk, and Ostend could only offer modest accommodation—and the same would apply in 1944. Cherbourg and Le Havre would be developed by subsequent generations but would never rival Antwerp. In 1805 Napoleon abandoned his plans of invading England to march east to defeat the Russians and Austrians at Austerlitz. During those same weeks, Trafalgar deprived him forever of being able to make any claim to command of the seas.

In 1914, when Germany invaded Belgium, the small country's army fell back on Antwerp as a last redoubt. The kaiser's troops laid siege to the port on September 26. Winston Churchill, then first lord of the Admiralty, became obsessed with the need to hang on to Antwerp, boldly setting up his own headquarters there. British troops also reinforced the garrison. But another unfortunate withdrawal ensued, and three British cruisers were lost when the city was surrendered on October 10. The following year, Churchill endeavored to profit from the lessons learned at Antwerp in an even more ambitious combined operation at Gallipoli. The results were proportionately still more disastrous.

Churchill became prime minister on May 10, 1940, the day the German blitzkrieg began in the West, and was horrified to witness helplessly the fall of Antwerp the following week. Already the previous November, as a member of Neville Chamberlain's cabinet, he had warned that any seizure by the *Wehrmacht* of Antwerp would "make it easier for them to carry out a mortal attack on this country." One of Churchill's own first cabinet directives on coming to power was to prepare demolition of the Antwerp docks and cranes. Like Napoleon before him, Hitler hastened to develop the port as one of the principal embarkation points for Operation Sealion, the projected invasion of Britain. This was the nearest in three major wars that Antwerp, once described by French military organizer Lazare Carnot as a pistol pointed at the heart of England, came to threatening Britain. But like Napoleon, Hitler was to abandon the project, and instead march eastward against Russia.

In all the massive planning for Opera-

German defenders surrendered Cherbourg on June 26, 1944, but not before thoroughly wrecking its harbor facilities, such as the railroad ferry terminal (above). The key Cotentin Peninsula port was not operational until the end of September. Germans similarly destroyed other ports along the English Channel coast.

tion Overlord that took place from the end of 1943 onward, Antwerp's possible significance in the Anglo-American invasion of northwest Europe barely gets a mention. In April-May 1944, General Montgomery, as land commander in chief, laid down his famous "Phase Lines." These prescribed an advance to the line of the Seine by D-plus-90. Thereafter, however, the planners had no clear objective defined; they certainly did not—as subsequent events show they should have done—target the need for a major port, i.e., Antwerp, for the next stage of the campaign against Germany. It was simply ignored by the Allied commander, General Eisenhower. No reference to Antwerp even appears in the copious diaries of Field Marshal Sir Alan Brooke, the cautious British chief of the Imperial General Staff whose role was to save Churchill from his worst strategic errors. According to Field Marshal Lord Bramall, then a subaltern in the 2nd King's Rifle Corps: "We hadn't projected that far ahead—we were convinced there was going to be a hard battle on the Seine, which there wasn't. When there wasn't, we felt the war was over and went flat out for Germany." (Bramall was Britain's last chief of the Defense Staff to have actually fought in Normandy.)

Certainly the planners had not reckoned on the huge logistical demands that their vast mechanized buildup would impose on the French road and rail system, shattered as it was by the Al-

lied bombing program, or on the realistic capacity of France's English Channel ports. Predicated on a logistical pause of one to two months, the British armies were to be supplied from those Channel ports, while the U.S. armies relied on Brittany's Brest and Normandy's Cherbourg, and later Marseilles, all very far from the battlefronts. If the Overlord planners did not see the problem, Hitler—the amateur strategist—certainly did, issuing draconian orders for all of the Channel ports to be heavily fortified and "to hold out to the last."

By the third week of June 1944, Lt. Gen. Joseph Lawton "Lightning Joe" Collins had pushed into the Cotentin Peninsula to invest the key port of Cherbourg—the first successful breakout from the D-Day beachhead. The Germans' die-hard defense of Cherbourg, however, was so successful that its docks were effectively destroyed, and the port would not be operational until the end of September, by which time the battle would have moved far to the east. By the end of July, Lt. Gen. George S. Patton had begun the breakout that would carry him right across France, and on August 22 the deadly Falaise trap closed around the remnants of the retreating German Seventh Army, killing ten thousand and taking fifty thousand prisoners. On the twentieth, Montgomery had been able to write triumphantly in his diary that the Battle of Normandy had been "decisively won." The Germans lost some 450,000 men, a tally comparable to that of Stalingrad. However, one entire army—General Hans von Salmuth's Fifteenth—had survived almost intact in the Pas de Calais area.

The Allies' brilliant Operation Fortitude deception plan—persuading Hitler until the last minute that Overlord was merely a feint, with the main attack coming in across the Strait of Dover—had successfully kept von Salmuth, with at least six of his original divisions, out of the battle. The commander, however, was sacked on August 25 because of his anti-Nazi sentiments and replaced by a dedicated National Socialist, Lt. Gen. Gustav-Adolf von Zangen. He now found the Fifteenth in danger of being trapped against the coast as Canadian troops advanced along the English Channel coast. Obeying Hitler's instructions to the letter, von Zangen turned each of the Channel ports into a mini-fortress, capable of resisting capture for many weeks, and then only surrendering when destruction was complete. Moreover, those units of the shattered German Seventh Army that had escaped the Falaise trap had remarkably managed to keep their formations together, with the officer cadres more or less intact, so that all twelve divisional commanders—plus their staffs—had gotten out and were able to re-form units. This was yet one more testimony to the high quality of the *Wehrmacht* even in defeat.

The battle surged toward Paris. Left to himself, Eisenhower would have been tempted to bypass it, but politics, humanitarian considerations, and the likelihood of Communist revolt in the city forced him to detach substantial forces, which entered it on August 25. The

Before the Germans could destroy the vital sluice gates and port installations at Antwerp, General Roberts' tanks had seized them.

British and Canadian troops of Montgomery's Twenty-first Army Group then thrust northeastward from the Seine. On September 3, the Guards Armored Division liberated Brussels. The next day, the British 11th Armored Division of Maj. Gen. G.P.B. "Pip" Roberts, in a brilliant coup, reached Antwerp itself. In the first of only two mentions of Antwerp in his diaries, the cautious Brooke exulted: "This evening our troops are reported in Brussels and advancing on Antwerp! It is very hard to believe it all!!"

Suddenly the port that for so many centuries had, in the wrong hands, seemed like a pistol pointing at Britain became, in the words of historian Maj. Gen. J.L. Moulton, "a pistol pointed at the heart of Germany." But would the Allies grasp it?

Before the Germans could destroy the vital sluice gates and port installations at Antwerp, General Roberts' tanks had seized them at the end of one of the fastest advances in history, in which the division had moved nonstop, sometimes all through the night. Men and vehicles

were fatigued but not exhausted. Roberts himself, nearly forty years later, insisted that resistance had still been so feeble that he could have gone on across the Albert Canal, which stretches from the Scheldt through northern Antwerp and eastward on to the Meuse River, had he not received orders from Montgomery to halt:

Monty's failure at Antwerp is evidence again that he was not a good general at seizing opportunities. My thoughts, like [Lt. Gen. Brian] Horrocks' and Monty's, on 4 September were east to the Rhine. We should have looked west towards Walcheren....

Unfortunately, I did not appreciate the significance of the fighting on the Albert Canal, and the Germans did not blow the crucial bridge [at Merksem] for another twelve hours. If briefed before, I would have crossed the Albert Canal with tanks to the east of Antwerp and closed the Germans' route into Beveland and Walcheren.

At that time petrol was coming up regularly on lorries, and we saved space on lorries by not using much ammunition. I had enough petrol to continue my advance.

Allied communiqués strongly gave the impression that the whole port of Antwerp, then the biggest in northwest Europe, as well as the one closest to Germany, now lay firmly in Allied hands. But in fact Antwerp straddles the wide mouth of the Scheldt River, with most of its harbor facilities on the north side of the Albert Canal, which remained in German hands, and the troops there were being swiftly reinforced. Most important, so long as the enemy controlled Antwerp's tortuous western water approaches, the island of Walcheren, and the semi-island of South Beveland, the great port itself was useless to the Allies. And, as Montgomery and Eisenhower were both beginning to realize, it was now urgently needed.

What had gone wrong? Could the port have been secured, following on the advance of the British 11th Armored Division?

General Horrocks, commander of the XXX Corps, which included the 11th Ar-

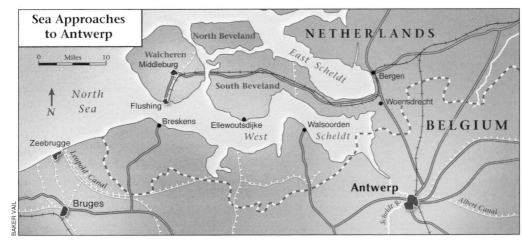

Sea Approaches to Antwerp

0   Miles   10

North Sea

NETHERLANDS

North Beveland

Walcheren
Middleburg

East Scheldt

South Beveland

Bergen

Woensdrecht

Flushing

Breskens   Ellewoutsdijke   Walsoorden

West   Scheldt   *Scheldt*

BELGIUM

Zeebrugge

Leopold Canal

Bruges

Antwerp

Scheldt R.   Albert Canal

BAKER VAIL

mored, reckoned that Roberts still had some one hundred miles of petrol per vehicle. But he had no orders to proceed farther. Instead of seizing the advantage and pushing northwestward across the Albert Canal and toward the vital isthmus of South Beveland less than twenty miles away, Roberts halted and vital time was lost.

The sudden appearance of Roberts' 11th Armored had evidently taken the German command at all levels totally by surprise. German General Count Stolberg zu Stolberg, the commander at Antwerp, told his captors that he had not expected them for several days. At his faraway headquarters in East Prussia, Hitler was struck with consternation that a seventy-mile gap now yawned along the Albert Canal from Antwerp to Hasselt and Maastricht. The door to western Germany stood ajar, and Hitler immediately ordered one of his best generals, the famous paratroop commander General Kurt Student, to fill the breach. Having been caught off balance, and now under draconian orders from the *Führer* (deserters were threatened with instant execution), the German army vigorously dug in behind the Albert Canal, even though most of the troops immediately available were so-called stomach invalids recuperating from fighting on the Russian Front. By the second week of September the immediate crisis for the Germans was over.

To a tank officer in the van of the Guards Armored Division, the future General

Because of the Allies' failure to secure Antwerp's approaches or any other large port intact, their supply situation became increasingly perilous as they raced across France. U.S. supplies were trucked from the Normandy beaches for hundreds of miles along the Red Ball Highway.

What was perhaps as serious as the failure to secure Antwerp was the escape of General von Zangen's Fifteenth Army across the Scheldt Estuary.

Sir David Fraser, "the awful suspicion began to dawn that the party was over." Heavy casualties came as an unexpected surprise. On September 6, Horrocks issued new orders for the 11th Armored

to forgo crossing the Albert Canal and instead swing eastward into Holland. This meant the end of any northwestward thrust.

What was perhaps equally as serious as the failure to secure Antwerp itself, if not more so, was the escape of General von Zangen's Fifteenth Army across the Scheldt Estuary. This was to have a serious effect on the next stage of the battle, the fight for Arnhem. The fall of Antwerp city, its tunnels, and ferries, had come as a stunning shock to von Zangen, who was pulling out along the Channel coast toward Holland, pursued by Lt. Gen. Henry Crerar's First Canadian Army, and ordered by Hitler to hold the Scheldt Estuary at all costs. The Germans' only supply and escape route now lay north across the West Scheldt Estuary and

then east via South Beveland, connected to the mainland by its narrow isthmus.

What followed was an extraordinary feat of improvisation, typical of the *Wehrmacht* at its best. Employing every available small coastal craft and moving by night so as to avoid Allied aircraft, von Zangen began transporting the bulk of his army from the Breskens pocket east of Zeebrugge across to South Beveland. It was something like a miniature Dunkirk, carried out in the teeth of Allied naval and air supremacy. Eventually, he succeeded in extricating more than eighty thousand fighting men, some of whom would soon appear, unexpectedly, under the ill-fated British airborne drop at Arnhem.

Horrocks later admitted that if he had "ordered Roberts [to] cross the Albert Canal and advance only fifteen miles to Woensdrecht, we should have blocked the Beveland isthmus." And Fraser, in his memoirs, conceded: "We had, I think, relaxed somewhat, lost impetus and I suspect there may have been a few days at the end of August when a sufficiently vigorous thrust somewhere, taking risks, remorselessly driven, might—conceivably—have kept the Germans on the run. Patton perhaps might have done it."

While Antwerp was being reached—and lost—on the Albert Canal, Supreme Headquarters Allied Expeditionary Force (SHAEF), amid much due celebration, was setting itself up in Paris and amid the splendors of Versailles. On September 1, Eisenhower had been promoted to not only supreme Allied commander but also commander of land forces, the post held by Montgomery from Overlord through the Normandy campaign. Monty could take solace in his promotion to field marshal, which is comparable to the U.S. rank of five-star general. Amid all the triumph of victory began the toughest, and in many ways most disagreeable, period of Eisenhower's career. He now had under him two

of the Allies' most awkward generals, Patton and Montgomery, ambitious and warring between themselves, each now determined to win the war his own way—and to corner all logistics to do so.

The simple Midwest farm boy in Eisenhower was infuriated by the excesses he found in Paris. Euphoria, or the so-called victory disease, had taken over in a big way and at all levels. What Carlo D'Este identified as an "unhealthy aura of overoptimism and self-deception" reigned. Similar intoxication affected Lt. Gen. Omar Bradley's Twelfth Army Group headquarters, and even Eisenhower himself was not immune. He was described, as late as mid-September, as being "euphoric about the prospects for an imminent ending of the war."

In Paris this unhealthy optimism was

also fueled by liquor, which was proving to be an acute problem with the U.S. forces there. Following the liberation, SHAEF's administrative chief, Lt. Gen. J.C.H. (nicknamed "Jesus Christ Himself") Lee, had moved eight thousand officers and twenty-one thousand men into the city, provoking the French to refer to SHAEF as "*Societé des Hoteliers Ameri-*

cans en France"! A disastrous appointment, Lee transported thousands of tons of prefabricated housing to keep his officers warm during the coming winter. Why Eisenhower kept Lee on remains a mystery; his demands on logistics, and his own incompetence, pointed up what had now become the most critical aspect of the war in northwest Europe—supply.

Because of the failure to open Cherbourg or the other Channel ports, all supplies for SHAEF's forces, then two million strong with 460,745 vehicles, still had to come across the Normandy beaches. Starting on August 26, to supply forces that were now several hundred miles to the east, six thousand trucks ferried supplies along the "Red Ball Highway," while a similar "Red Lion Express" supplied the Twenty-first Army

Group with five hundred tons a day off the same beaches. Inevitably, the carriers themselves consumed a good proportion of the vital fuel they were transporting. A thriving black market accounted for the loss of additional fuel. It was calculated that one U.S. division required an average of seven hundred tons per day in combat (the drawbacks of modern mechanized

Soldiers of the First Canadian Army riding aboard jeeps and troop carriers enter the outskirts of Rouen, France, on August 30. Forming the left flank of the British Twenty-first Army Group's northeastward advance from the Seine, the Canadians were tasked with capturing fortresslike Channel ports.

IMPERIAL WAR MUSEUM

warfare and a vehicle-bound army), while the average German division—many of which were horse-drawn—could survive on two hundred tons.

As the front moved farther east, British supplies had to come four hundred miles from Bayeux, while the Germans were less than sixty miles from the Third Reich's industrial heartland—the Ruhr. And then Paris alone, with hungry Jesus Christ Himself Lee aboard, demanded a minimum of twenty-four hundred tons a day. Even when Cherbourg's port was cleared at the end of September, the round trip to supply the U.S. armies totaled more than seven hundred miles and took a truck seventy-one hours to complete.

All Allied strategies were now dependent entirely on "the tyranny of supply." And by this time the days of great opportunity for the Allies were over.

Already on August 24, Eisenhower, though himself optimistic about an early end to the war, was warning U.S. Army Chief of Staff George C. Marshall that his armies did not have sufficient supplies "to do everything that we should like to do." By this he meant fulfill the rival designs of both Patton and Montgomery with which he was currently being bombarded. SHAEF, meanwhile, had failed to propose its own logistical plans for "dealing with success on such an epic scale."

The ascetic, nonsmoking teetotaler Montgomery was then at his forward headquarters in Belgium. By mid-August his relations with Eisenhower regarding further prosecution of the war had become strained. On September 3, Montgomery sent a top-secret instruction, Directive M523, to the Twenty-first Army Group declaring his intention "to occupy the Ruhr." The eastward advance would begin on the sixth, and the directive predicted, "The Armies of the Allies will soon be entering Germany." From this it was apparent that Montgomery, too, had by then become somewhat infected by the widespread victory disease, and he was not anticipating heavy resistance. That same day, talks took place between Lt. Gen. Miles Dempsey, commander of the British Second Army, and Maj. Gen. Maxwell Taylor of the U.S. 101st Airborne Division about seizing a bridge

Left: Although Field Marshal Alan Brooke, chief of the Imperial General Staff, exulted in the capture of Antwerp, he apparently failed to see the need to make the seizure of its approaches a high priority. Right: Lieutenant General Brian Horrocks commanded the British XXX Corps.

across the Rhine (in Holland) at Arnhem and a span over the Waal River at Nijmegen. An unrealistically early date was fixed—September 8-9.

On September 4, Montgomery sent Eisenhower an important strategic summary urging "one really powerful and full-blooded thrust toward Berlin" to end the war, followed with the qualification (with which Patton would have been fully in accord): "We have not enough maintenance resources for two full-blooded thrusts." Monty's thrust was to be in the north, led by him, and composed of the British Twenty-first Army Group. Even if Montgomery had not by now gained a reputation with the Americans for being so abrasive, with U.S. forces then gaining a preponderance of more than 2-to-1 on the ground, politically his proposition would have been unacceptable. Furthermore, the supplies then available (without Antwerp) would almost certainly have proven to be quite inadequate to safely maintain even one single thrust of forty divisions, as proposed by Montgomery, with the Germans fighting in their own backyard. On September 7, he fired off an urgent plea to Eisenhower that underlined the problem:

My maintenance is stretched to the limit. I require an air lift of 1,000 tons a day at Douai or Brussels and in last two days have had only 750 tons total. My transport is based on operating 150 miles from my ports and at present I am over 300 miles from Bayeux. In order to save transport I have cut down my

intake into France to 6,000 tons a day which is half what I consume and I cannot go on for long like this. It is clear therefore that based as I am at present on Bayeux I cannot capture the Ruhr.

Monty repeated an urgent request for the supreme commander to "come and see me." Identical howls about supplies were also landing simultaneously on Eisenhower's desk from Bradley and Patton. It should have been quite clear (at least so Montgomery thought) that unless the Germans really were on their last legs, an early two-pronged attack across the Rhine would be logistically impossible. Predictably, Patton reinforced his requests by getting his Third Army locked into costly and futile attacks on Metz so that Eisenhower would be forced to divert more supplies to him.

Clearly only Antwerp would have filled the bill, but still its capture was not listed as a top priority. On August 17, when efforts had dragged on to close the Falaise Gap, Montgomery's personal diaries reveal him putting to Bradley the need for the Twenty-first Army Group to "secure Antwerp." The following day this was followed up in a Montgomery-to-Brooke dispatch in which Monty used the same words and also wrote of "future plans." He had noted that "Bradley agrees entirely," but that he had "NOT yet discussed subject with IKE." On the twenty-eighth, Montgomery was formulating plans for an airdrop on Tournai, with its objective "to seize the line of the Scheldt." The speed of the advance on Brussels and Antwerp was to preempt this plan.

Equally, on September 21, U.S. Lt. Gen. Lewis Brereton, commander of the First Allied Airborne Army, finally vetoed an early September proposal by Montgomery to drop the force on heavily defended Walcheren Island. A singularly unimpressive figure, the hedonistic Brereton was rated by Bradley as only "marginally competent" and dedicated to "living in the biggest French chateau." In early September he had at his disposal, however, on seven days' notice, the whole British 1st Airborne Division and the Polish Para Brigade. Montgomery meanwhile stated that no clear directive was forthcoming from Eisenhower or Brooke to make the capture of Antwerp and its approaches a top priority. Eisenhower's biographer, Stephen Ambrose, holding the supreme commander "ultimately responsible," admitted that Ike was seen to waver here—and badly—presumably because euphoria about impending German collapse momentarily made the port seem superfluous.

Eisenhower, endeavoring to escape the counterproductive mood prevailing in Paris, had moved his headquarters back to isolated Granville, south of Cherbourg on the Cotentin Peninsula. Understandable as his motives were, it was a disastrous choice, and especially at so critical a point in the campaign. For the first three crucial weeks of September, until Eisenhower decided to move to Versailles, communications with SHAEF at Granville were, according to D'Este, "dangerously ineffective" and in fact occasionally disrupted. To make matters worse, Eisenhower had wrenched his knee and was suffering considerable pain, which affected his temper, if not his judgment. Acceding to Monty's requests, on September 10 he flew to Brussels to meet him. Ike's discomfort was such that he could not get out of the plane; conse-

No clear directive was forthcoming to make the capture of Antwerp and its approaches a top priority.

quently, the discussions had to take place inside it. The tempers of both men were strained to a breaking point. In Ambrose's account, the meeting ended with Eisenhower allegedly having "leaned forward and put his hand on Montgomery's knee. 'Steady, Monty,' he said. 'You can't speak to me like that. I'm your boss.' Montgomery mumbled that he was sorry."

About all that emerged from this acerbic meeting between the two commanders was Eisenhower's endorsement of Montgomery's plan to seize the bridges at Nijmegen and Arnhem—the fateful Operation Market-Garden. Its date was now fixed—at greatest speed—for September 17, just a week ahead. Mont-

gomery agreed with Lt. Gen. Frederick "Boy" Browning, the First Allied Airborne Army's deputy commander, and Dempsey that the whole force would have to be thrown in because "enemy resistance there is getting stronger." Von Zangen had by now already managed to transport a large part of his Fifteenth Army across the Scheldt. According to Monty's chief of intelligence, Brig. Gen. Bill Williams, the British commander was convinced that if Market-Garden succeeded in establishing a bridgehead across the Rhine, "Eisenhower would be bound to reinforce success." Illustrative of the extreme coolness that by now had set in between the two, Eisenhower's follow-up letter on the fifteenth was addressed with an icy "Dear Montgomery." For the rest of the war, their relations would grow progressively remoter, their personal encounters fewer.

The pros and cons of tragic Arnhem have been debated ad nauseam: the gung-ho determination of the airborne army (equally suffering from the victory disease) to get into the war after seventeen aborted operations; the faulty plan-

British paratroopers move through a destroyed building in Oosterbeek, Holland, during Operation Market-Garden, Montgomery's ambitious attempt to establish a bridgehead across the Rhine River. No effort, meanwhile, was made to clear the Scheldt Estuary of Germans.

IMPERIAL WAR MUSEUM

ning; the optimistic disregard of adverse intelligence reports; the long, painfully vulnerable single causeway along which Horrocks' armor had to advance; the poor wireless communications; the lack of fighter-bomber support; the remarkable fighting power displayed, once again, by the German defenders; the landing of the British paras too far from the crucial bridge, a "Bridge too Far"; and so forth. But perhaps no less significant was the role played in the battle by the presence of von Zangen's men under the Allied airdrop. Might not the battle have gone differently had they been kept bottled up on the far side of the Scheldt, as they would have been if the British tanks could have reached South Beveland on September 4?

Most relevant of all, however, was the fact that Montgomery's concentration on Arnhem, his fixation to "bounce the Germans back over the Rhine" and reach the Ruhr in one fell swoop, meant that he was now looking in the wrong direction, away from securing the port essential to prosecuting the next stage of the war. David Fraser, then a tank commander in the Guards Armored thrust down the Nijmegen road, commented: "The flaw in Market-Garden was not inadequate logistic support for Eisenhower's left, but inadequate appreciation of the fact that even if the bridges at Nijmegen and Arnhem had been taken, the line of communication could not support the subsequent campaign without a functioning port of Antwerp. What was required, therefore, was a campaign to open Scheldt as a pre-requisite to further operations." With the distance of hindsight, one well may ask, if not for Eisenhower and Montgomery's fundamental incompatibility, would Arnhem or the Ardennes have ever happened?

Who was immediately to blame—Eisenhower or Montgomery? One needs to look at the sequence of orders and signals. As already noted, prior to Montgomery's ex-

change with Bradley on August 17, there had been no significant mention of Antwerp in Allied high command orders. On September 4, the same day Montgomery had sent Eisenhower his bombshell about a "single thrust," Eisenhower sent him and other subordinate commanders a dispatch beginning: "Enemy resistance on the entire front shows signs of collapse....The mission of Northern Group of Armies and of that part of Central Group of Armies operating north-west of the Ardennes is to secure Antwerp, breach the sector of the Siegfried Line covering the Ruhr and then seize the Ruhr."

However, as Major L.F. Ellis put it in the official *British History of the Second World War*: "There was nothing in the wording of the directive to show that the use of Antwerp, involving the freedom of the Scheldt, was of any special or pressing importance." Nor would Montgomery have interpreted the directive as an order setting the Scheldt as a top priority. Meanwhile, the British commander already had his sights fixed on the more ambitious goal of Arnhem.

On September 13, Eisenhower followed up his dispatch of the fourth with another wordy message, stating, "I am

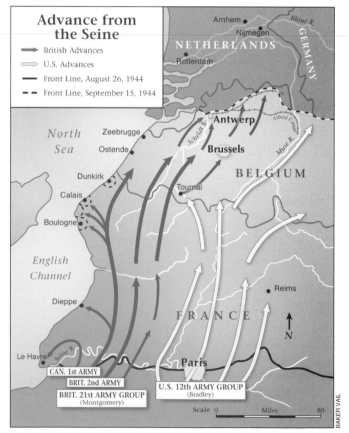

Advance from the Seine

→ British Advances
⇨ U.S. Advances
— Front Line, August 26, 1944
--- Front Line, September 15, 1944

Arnhem
Nijmegen
Rhine R.
NETHERLANDS
Rotterdam
GERMANY

North Sea
Zeebrugge
Ostende
Antwerp
Scheldt R.
Albert Canal
Brussels
Dunkirk
Calais
Tournai
BELGIUM
Meuse R.
Boulogne

English Channel
Dieppe
Reims

FRANCE
Paris

Le Havre
Seine R.
N

CAN. 1st ARMY
BRIT. 2nd ARMY
U.S. 12th ARMY GROUP
(Bradley)
BRIT. 21st ARMY GROUP
(Montgomery)
Scale 0   Miles   80

BAKER VAIL

confirmed in my previously expressed conviction that the early winning of deep water ports and improved maintenance facilities in our rear are prerequisites to a final all-out assault on Germany proper."

Again, hardly a definite order. Seven days later, by which time Market-Garden had started and was floundering, an Eisenhower message repeated as a "prerequisite" the "early capture of the approaches to Antwerp." Only by the twenty-ninth was he expressing this objective (to the Combined Chiefs of Staff) as a "matter of transcendent importance."

On October 8, Montgomery received the following message from Eisenhower: "Plans of both Army Groups must retain as first mission the gaining of the line of the Rhine north of Bonn as quickly as humanly possible." The following day, however, another message from Ike came through, noting, "The recent gale has materially reduced the intake at Cherbourg while Arromanches, which we counted on to assist materially in supply for U.S. forces, has been severely damaged." The Allied commander declared in much more urgent terms that unless Antwerp was functioning by the middle of November, "All operations will come to a standstill. I must emphasize that, of all our operations on our entire front from Switzerland to the channel, I consider Antwerp of first importance."

By the thirteenth, a clearly impatient Eisenhower was adopting a tougher line with Montgomery, explaining the critical supply situation of all his armies, and then acidly adding, "If you could have a similarly clear picture of that situation you would understand why I keep reverting again and again to the matter of getting Antwerp into a workable condition."

Three days later, Montgomery responded: "I have given Antwerp top priority in all operations in 21 Army Group and all energies and efforts will now be devoted toward opening up that place. Your very devoted and loyal subordinate." Eisenhower fired one last shot, on October 28:

"The securing and placing in operation of that port [Antwerp] is our first and most important immediate objective." It was late in the game, if not too late.

If Eisenhower was impatient, his Allied naval commander, Admiral Sir Bertram Ramsay, was positively fuming. Of all the senior Allied brass, Ramsay seems to have been the most aware of the importance of Antwerp. On September 4, the very day that the 11th Armored reached the harbor, Ramsay had signaled SHAEF, "It is essential if Antwerp and Rotterdam are to be opened quickly enemy must be prevented from…mining and blocking Scheldt."

The following day, the admiral wrote in his diary, "Antwerp is useless unless the Scheldt estuary is cleared of the enemy." He went on to record how disturbed he was "at the lack of preparation" to that end. "The Armies are hung up in their advance by outrunning their supplies." By September nearly all the Channel ports, including Le Havre, Dieppe, and Boulogne, had been captured from the land side. Most of their equipment, however, had been systematically destroyed. In contrast, on flying to Antwerp shortly after Roberts' capture of the port, Ramsay "was most impressed by the vast extent of them—numberless cranes undamaged."

The admiral fiercely criticized the failure to plan a forward operation against the Antwerp approaches. No provision had been made at supreme headquarters for such an operation, no amphibious force was ready, and nearly all the U.S. assault landing craft had been sent to the Mediterranean, for the invasion of Southern France, or to the Far East.

On September 14, Ramsay visited Montgomery to press for priority to be given for the opening of Antwerp. After Arnhem, he returned to the charge with even greater vigor, but his opinion carried little weight, as by then he no longer had an amphibious striking force at his disposal. On the thirtieth, he flew to meet with Eisenhower, whom he found "a little depressed." The admiral impressed upon him "that the Army

Admiral Sir Bertram Ramsay (left) was the only Allied senior commander who grasped the importance of quickly capturing Antwerp's approaches, writing on September 5, the port "is useless unless the Scheldt estuary is cleared of the enemy."

[was] underestimating the magnitude of the operation for the capture of Walcheren." On October 1, Ramsay repeated in his diary his "great anxiety about Walcheren. I think the Army [i.e., Montgomery] is not taking this operation seriously enough, and I see I shall have to do something to make them."

Four days later, at a high-level meeting at SHAEF at Versailles, Ramsay was deeply shocked. He wrote:

Monty made the startling announcement that we could take the Ruhr without Antwerp. This afforded me the cue I needed to lambast him for not having made the capture of Antwerp the immediate objective at highest priority, and I let fly with all my guns at the faulty strategy we had allowed. Our large forces were now practically grounded for lack of supply….CIGS Brooke told me after the meeting that I had spoken his thoughts and that it was high time somebody expressed them.

Of that October 5 meeting at Versailles, Brooke noted in his diary—and this was his only mention of the Antwerp issue: "I feel that Monty's strategy for once is at fault, instead of carrying out the advance on Arnhem he ought to

have made certain of Antwerp in the first place. Ramsay brought this out well in discussion and criticised Monty freely. Ike nobly took all blame on himself as he had approved Monty's suggestion to operate on Arnhem."

On October 23, Ramsay received a message from Montgomery, criticizing him for dealing directly with Crerar, the Canadian army commander, over Walcheren: "I replied that I had done so all along because of his [Montgomery's] seeming reluctance to concern himself….The fact is that it has at last come home that Antwerp is the first priority of all, and he has moved back to Brussels to give it his attention. And high time too."

Back on October 16, Montgomery had at last ordered that the Twenty-first Army Group concentrate on Antwerp, but six precious weeks had been lost. His explanation was that, all along, he continued to believe he could carry on with his main effort toward the Ruhr and that the valiant and seriously extended—Canadians could deal with the clearing of the Scheldt in a subsidiary operation. He had not reckoned on the resoluteness of the German defenders, and the effectiveness, even at this late stage in the war, of the *Führer*'s orders for fanatical last-ditch resistance. He also did not consider the slowness on the part of the Canadians to mount the kind of major amphibian operation required. In addition, there was the repeated refusal of Brereton—right through October—to assist with an airborne operation on South Beveland.

So who was to blame? While British historians such as Richard Lamb, Corelli Barnett, and Maj. Gen. J.L. Moulton blame Montgomery principally for the failure at Antwerp, American historians such as Carlo D'Este, Stephen Ambrose, and Roger Cirillo are more generous, placing a large portion of the blame on Eisenhower. In my opinion there was culpable neglect at all levels from Roosevelt and Churchill down. But it is on the supreme Allied commander's desk that the buck chiefly has to rest. Eisenhower should have seen the crucial importance of Antwerp back in May 1944, and from

LEFT: NATIONAL ARCHIVES; ABOVE: AFTER THE BATTLE

The British operation to clear the approaches to the Scheldt finally began in early November. Left: Canadians prepare amphibious Buffaloes for an assault across the West Scheldt. Above: British Commandos move through Flushing on Walcheren Island.

September on, his orders to Montgomery should have been far more categorical.

At the risk of falling into the pernicious trap of hindsight, how could Eisenhower and Montgomery between them have done it better? With the sudden collapse of the German front at the end of August, almost certainly a thrust by a reinforced 11th Armored Division could have pushed on the extra twenty miles over the Albert Canal, to seize Bergen and seal off South Beveland by September 4. General Roberts and his supporters reckoned that one fresh infantry brigade and an extra tank brigade could have done the trick. But they would have been hard-pressed to hold it against an inevitable German counterattack and would have to have been swiftly backed up. Why not by a strong flying column, earmarked specifically for that very task? And why not simultaneously by a major airborne drop into South Beveland and Walcheren Island itself in order to take the heavy gun positions there from the rear while the Germans were still unprepared?

Brereton's refusal should have been overruled. Yes, many British and Canadian paratroops did lose their lives on D-Day, drowning after landing in areas flooded by the Germans close to the Dives River in Normandy. And when the Canadians and British Commandos finally assaulted Walcheren in November, the Germans' flooding of the island made

their task especially difficult. But was the terrain all that different from the Arnhem-Nijmegen area? The element of shock while the Germans were still off balance in early September would have been immense. For Brereton, the coastal flak was also an inhibiting factor. The airborne leaders both at Arnhem and Wesel used the same arguments. On the Scheldt approaches, however, the gun batteries were concentrated in a much smaller area, and therefore should have been easier to smother in the kind of heavy preliminary bombing and naval shelling that preceded D-Day. As noted earlier, the airborne was raring to go, and a South Beveland–Bergen operation could have been carried out on a far smaller scale than Nijmegen-Arnhem. Its success would have made Arnhem either unnecessary or given it infinitely better prospects of subsequent victory.

On September 10, according to Major Ellis, Eisenhower ought to have ordered Montgomery "that not another day should be lost before Twenty-First Army Group freed Antwerp port." And this was despite the fact that Eisenhower himself admitted to having clearly seen the cogent need to use Antwerp.

The long-neglected operation to clear the approaches to the Scheldt finally got underway on November 1, 1944. It was what the Canadian official historian appropriately called a "Cinderella battle," one of the nastiest fights of the entire war in northwestern Europe, involving

British Commandos and Royal Marines, but primarily troops of the First Canadian Army. In one small glimpse of it, the official historian of the Canadian 3rd Division recorded: "The fighting in the Breskens Pocket was marked by the utter misery of the conditions and the great courage required to do the simplest things. Attacks had to go along dykes swept by enemy fire. To go through the polders [land reclaimed from sea] meant wading, without possibility of concealment, in water that at times came up to the chest."

Twice more, Brereton turned down requests for airborne support. Finally, on November 28, after a costly mine-clearing operation involving 150 minesweepers, Antwerp was opened to shipping. Eighty-five days after the British 11th Armored had captured the port, an ecstatic populace greeted a first convoy of nineteen Liberty ships. By the end of 1944, an average of 13,700 tons of supplies a day was being unloaded for the Americans, and eighty-six hundred for the British. (By comparison, the combined tonnage handled by Marseilles and Toulon totaled only thirteen thousand tons per day.)

The price had been heavy. In the bombing of the town of Westkapelle alone, 198 Dutch civilians were killed; in Antwerp itself a total of 1,214 of Hitler's V-weapons landed indiscriminately on the city, killing three thousand civilians and seriously injuring another twelve thousand. Allied losses totaled 703 officers and 12,170 other ranks killed, wounded, and missing, of whom half were Canadian.

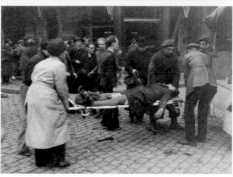

Counted in the cost of the lost opportunity at Antwerp should perhaps also be the nearly eighty thousand Americans who fell in Hitler's surprise Ardennes offensive that was launched on December 16 and whose objective was the recapture of Antwerp. Hitler, if not SHAEF, realized the full value of the port—that once it was in full operation the Reich was inexorably doomed to full-scale invasion from the west. With SHAEF slumbering amid the delights of Paris, still afflicted by the victory disease and preparing for Christmas, the Allies were caught thoroughly off balance. It was a crazy gamble such as only a doomed madman like Hitler could have attempted. The Ardennes offensive nevertheless got halfway to its goal. One contributory factor to the disaster on the American side undoubtedly was the shortage of supplies attributable to the blocking of Antwerp. The attack caused serious panic both among the Belgian population and at SHAEF, disrupting and postponing plans for the coming final offensive into Germany. But for the heroic defense of the encircled GIs at Bastogne and elsewhere, Allied air supremacy once the weather had cleared, and the speed of Patton's legendary 90-degree turnaround, it remains just possible—though improbable—that Hitler's bid for the high stake of Antwerp might have paid off.

At least the German attempt illustrated the value of Antwerp and the historic folly of the Allies in not giving the securing of the port and its approaches the highest priority in their pre–D-Day deliberations. It was a failure that opens up all kinds of speculation to the imaginative historian—such as, with Antwerp opened in September 1944, might we yet have gotten to Berlin before Stalin did? Had the war, in consequence, possibly ended before the close of the year, as Ike had once wagered Monty, how many lives in the concentration camps, not to mention the German civilians of Dresden, might have been saved?

ALISTAIR HORNE is an *MHQ* contributing editor and the author of many military history books, including *Monty: The Lonely Leader 1944-1945* (HarperCollins, 1994), *The Age of Napoleon* (Random House, April 2004), and a forthcoming history of France (Knopf).

Top: Residents mill about a market in Antwerp's city square, in a prewar photograph. The Allies' failure to quickly open Antwerp to supply traffic perhaps cost them their best chance to end the war in 1944. The city suffered heavily from a byproduct of that failure: destruction wrought by German V-weapons. Rescue workers search through rubble (above) after a V-2 strike on the city and hurry off a girl wounded in the attack (right).

EXPERIENCE OF WAR

Pinned Down Outside Port Hudson

Edited by Richard G. Latture

Most soldiers writing home spare their families the horror of what they endure in battle. John B. Whitehead, however, was an exception. Possessing a keen eye for detail, the Union private described to his wife, Mary, and children the disease and death that pervaded his camp and the battlefield outside Confederate-held Port Hudson, Louisiana. Moreover, he wanted his one and only battle experience to serve as a warning to his neighbors.

At the ripe age of thirty-eight, the Washington, Connecticut, farmer had signed up for nine months' service in Company D, 28th Connecticut Infantry, on September 8, 1862. After receiving accouterments and weapons, "good Enfield rifles," while encamped at Centreville Course on Long Island, New York, the 28th embarked on the steam transport Che Kiang in early December prior to heading south. About fourteen hundred soldiers were packed onto the vessel, and Whitehead got his first taste of military hardship before they left the harbor. On December 3, he wrote to his family:

We were so full we could not get a place large enough to lie down in. I sat up all night Sunday night. Monday night I had a good place. I lay on the table in the dining room. Many lay on the floor where the tobacco spittle and other filth was too nasty for hogs to lie in. Every place large enough for a man to lie in was taken up and many went out where there was nothing but the heavens above them and lay all night....

John Whitehead, like many Civil War soldiers, experienced a religious conversion while in the army, his awakening coming after Che Kiang was buffeted off the south Atlantic coast by a "perfect gale that we hardly lived through." On December 11, he wrote his wife that "God is to be praised for preserving our lives through this voyage when he alone could save us....He shall have the affection of my heart while I live, and Mary, I feel that you have almost been persuaded to be a Christian, that I have kept you back, but I will do it no longer."

After landing near the mouth of the Mississippi River on December 12, the 28th Connecticut was stationed in and around Pensacola, Florida, where its relatively quiet service was highlighted by a fruitless early March foray against Confederate guerrillas.

In his letters home, Private Whitehead recounted that and other adventures, gave some fatherly advice to his oldest son, Edwin ("I don't think there is any harm in playing cards for amusement, if we don't let it interfere with our other duties"), and repeated verse he found on Southern tombstones, "which show although they are rebels, they worshipped the same god we do." But he always wrote of his desire to return home.

On May 10, Whitehead and the 28th embarked on transports, and fifteen days later landed eight miles from Port Hudson. The next day, Union Maj. Gen. Nathaniel Banks' Army of the Gulf laid siege to the bastion, which overlooked the Mississippi.

The Confederate garrison easily repulsed an uncoordinated May 27 attack. In a July 1, 1863, letter to his family, Private Whitehead recounted the second, June 14, assault, in which some six thousand Federal troops charged sections of the works defended by 3,750 Rebels. Union losses totaled almost eighteen hundred versus only forty-seven Confederate casualties. Port Hudson finally surrendered on July 9. John Whitehead was honorably discharged from the army on August 28, 1863, and returned to farming.

Dear ones at home,

Yesterday I got four letters from you and one from sister Mary which made one hour pass pleasantly in this dark time. I am not very well and not very sick. Have done nothing in a week but am getting better. I think I shall be returned to duty in a day or two. Every word any of you write is highly prized.

We are not very pleasantly situated here. We have had no tents of any kind since we left Brashear City most six weeks ago. We carry nothing with us except a rubber blanket, overcoat, haversack, and canteen. Some of the time we are in one place and then in another. We are lying around in the rear of Port Hudson to keep those in that are in and the rebs out that are out. Our men made an attack on their works Sunday, June 14th. We were not successful. Eleven men from each Co. in our regt. were with the advance; the rest were farther back. We lost from our regt. 60 killed, wounded, and missing. Capt. Hoag was killed which is a loss to this Co. that can't be made up. Charles Bemas has not been found. The chances that he is alive are very small. Charles Wooding was badly wounded; some of our Co. slightly. Four from our Co. have enlisted for two years. Jay Ferris died in New Orleans. We left him there. When we were coming up the River[,] Noxen Kinney died.

Alexander Conkright was alive and like to get well the last we heard from him. I don't know whether Jo Crane is dead or alive; we hear so many stories. So many have died and we have left so many sick at different places that 4 reenlisting leaves our Co. very small. We have not but 16 men fit for duty. Lieut. Booth is sick at Baton Rouge. Lieut. Hungerford is sick here, so J. Logan is the first officer on duty, and he can't but just crawl about. It is the climate; the sun is most directly over our heads. The three years men that were in this climate last year so they got used to it, look healthy and they are....

Corp. Marsh had a fever and might [not] have died with good treatment, but there was an old Dr. got in the Regt. about that

A portion of the formidable Confederate defenses at Port Hudson, Louisiana. During a June 1863 attack, John Whitehead and other Federals were pinned down outside the works for almost twenty-four hours.

time and proscribed for him. He proscribed 30 drops of tincture of wolfsbane which they had never had. They had the extract so it was delt out to him, and two drops would have been a large dose. It began to affect him as soon as he took it and like to have killed him right off. They got the other doctor as soone as they could. He gave him an emetic, and got as much off his stomach as he could, but he did not get over it. I think he lived about one week. The old Dr. was drunk when he proscribed for him....

I am now going to write some things which I should not if I know I should live to come home to tell them. As longe as I am alive I expect to come home, but still I may not. Life is uncertain anywhere, but more so here.

Sunday morning, June 14th, we were called up 2 o'clock to get breakfast, and just at daylight we were marched on to the battle field. We were not the advance; there were several regt. ahead of us so by the time we got within a mile of the rebel works, they began to fetch the wounded and dying back by us in a constant stream, and many came back alone, some with only one finger gone, some two, some the hand all tore to pieces, in short, wounded in most all parts of body and limb. Those that could walk did, and others were brought off. We were marched within 15 or 20 rods of the rebels breast work in a shower of bullets and were ordered to fall which we did right in the road under cover of a small bank from one to two feet high which sheltered us from the enemy's bullets some. They were shooting oure men from behind their breast works so we could not see them. They probably shot 50 of oure men to oure shooting one of theirs.

We lay there in the road from sunrise till dark with the sun passing allmost verticle over our heads. It was a bright clear day and quite a number got so dry and warm they tride to get out and got shot. If a man raised his head he most assuredly got shot. We lay there and saw many a man get shot, some shot so dead they never stirred after they fell; others so they limped and crawled off; others lay and died in the hot sun within two or three rods of us, and we could not lift a hand to help them. The last of the wounded they tried to get off. For every one they got off, the two that were trying to get them off got wounded so they had to give it up.

We lay in that place till Monday morning about day-light when we were drawn back. We had a good many killed [and] wounded that lay close up to their breastworks. They would not let us get them to bury or take care of the wounded till Tues-day afternoon. When we came in Monday morning those that were killed were covered with maggots and smelt so we couldn't stay by them. They had been dead about 24 hours. All the wounded that could crawl away did so; those that could not had to ly in that boiling sun and die by inches, covered with maggots before they were dead, till Tuesday afternoon when they gave us a chance to bury the dead. Even then two men were found alive but crazy, with their ears full of maggots.

These are facts I have written, but you need not make much noise about it. I hope Hubbell will keep his boys out of it just as long as he can legally. I don't know as I had ought to have written anything about this, but I wanted you and Edwin to know it. I thought perhaps Hubbell would try a little harder to keep his boys; I should hate to have them get into this war. If they have to go they must do the best they can and we must help them all we can, but I want them kept out as long as they can be. You can show this to him; if he thinks you had better not show it to any one else, you can keep it to yourself.

I got the money, comb, and flowers which you sent. I liked to see the flowers. Mary, if I don't dream of you nights it is not because I don't think of you day times for you are all on my mind when awake. I am broke of sleep a good deal so when I sleep I sleep sound. I think if I live a few weeks longer I shall start for home. I am not down hearted or discouraged but am looking for the time when I shall see you all again.

J.B.W.

RICHARD G. LATTURE is the associate editor of *MHQ*.

After besieging Saragossa for more than a month, on

January 27, 1809, a French army finally breached the

Spanish city's fortifications—then the real battle began.

Spain's HORRIFIC and HEROIC Siege

by Jonathan North   The twenty-seventh of January 1809 dawned drab and

dismal. A light mist seemed to hang in the air, but the cold of the Spanish winter was in-

tense. French troops huddled in the trenches before Saragossa, chatting nervously and shak-

ing themselves to keep warm. Napoleon's soldiers had been encamped before the Spanish city

for more than a month, enduring the wearisome monotony of siege warfare, fervently hop-

ing for a breakthrough that might finish the ordeal. But the Spanish defenders were in no

mood to capitulate. The silence of the early morning was occasionally broken by the sharp

crack of a sniper's musket. Some of the balls whistled harmlessly overhead; others thudded

into the breastworks of the French trenches. Soon that noise was drowned by the boom of

French siege guns, their massive round shot directed against the city's ancient defenses.

Colonel Josef Chlopiski exhorts the 1st Vistula Regiment to advance through a breach in the wall of the Santa Engracia Convent during the French army's January 27, 1809, assault against Saragossa. Spanish defenders, meanwhile, pepper the attackers with musket fire.

By 10 A.M. the bulk of a French assault force had gathered. The brusque General Pierre Habert inspected his veterans, moving through the ranks, encouraging and cajoling. In the center, a Major Stahl and three hundred *voltigeurs* prepared to attack a breach in the city wall that had been pounded open by the French siege guns. On the right, a second column formed up to assault the guns on a Spanish parapet—the Palafox Battery, named after the defenders' illustrious commander. A third column, led by Colonel Josef Chlopiski and composed of Poles from the 1st Vistula Regiment, was to attack the Santa Engracia Convent, which formed part of the city's southern wall.

At 11 A.M. the gigantic French guns directed their fire against the city itself. The defenders had virtually ceased firing, perhaps waiting for the French, perhaps too busy bolstering ruined walls with sacks of earth. Then, at noon, was heard the signal for which the entire French army had been anxiously waiting: Three field guns opened fire, one after the other. The French and their allies clambered noisily out of their trenches and began to run forward across the frosty ground. Spaniards opened fire from the walls, and here and there Frenchmen and Poles were hit and fell. Sensing victory, the rest pushed forward. But before they could reach the breach, Stahl's men were hit by canister fire and counterattacked by a strong force of seven hundred Spaniards. The *voltigeurs* reeled from the shock and scattered. Some ran back to the trenches; others fought hand to hand with their assailants.

The second column was more fortunate, bursting through the breach into Pabostre Avenue, where the greatcoated Frenchmen barricaded themselves inside some battered houses. Throwing beams across doorways and furniture against windows, they fiercely resisted as Spanish reserves counterattacked and vainly swarmed around them.

Chlopiski's four companies also vigorously attacked, but were astonished to find a second wall had been built behind the breach in the convent wall. Spanish soldiers positioned on the terraces of nearby buildings rained down musket fire. Undeterred, the Poles forced their way through a tiny gap in this unexpected ten-foot-high obstacle, broke into the convent, and took on its twelve hundred defenders. A Spaniard smashed Baron Louis François Lejeune in the face with his musket butt. The French engineer officer was dazed but still managed to mentally record the infernal scene before being wounded again "by a ricocheting bullet in the shoulder, causing…tremendous pain." Like "furious lions," the Poles clawed their way through the convent's church before breaking out into the little square behind the building. As the attackers began to occupy the neighboring houses, Spaniards along the wall found themselves cut off and turned to face the new threat.

The French 5th Light Regiment, meanwhile, rose from its trenches, dashed forward, and scaled the city wall, along which Spanish cannons were arrayed. Supported by the 115th Line Regiment, the 5th pushed on to capture fifteen guns and penetrate as far as the Trinitarian Convent. But for the regiments the cost was high: forty-three dead and 136 wounded. Even so, they were within the walls. Overall, the French assault that day had been a success, and the Spanish city, by rights, should now have capitulated. But Saragossa was no ordinary city, and this was no ordinary war.

O n the afternoon of Friday, November 4, 1808, Napoleon Bonaparte had crossed the Pyrenees Mountains and entered the kingdom of Spain. He and his veteran army had come to restore his empire's fortunes in that country, where a popular revolt was threatening the rule of Napoleon's elder brother, King Joseph.

Earlier that year, Napoleon, an old hand at deciding the fate of nations and monarchs, had deposed the old Bourbon dynasty and installed Joseph on the throne. In the summer of 1808, the Spanish people fought back. The French, victorious in battle against Spain's regular forces, could never overcome popular resistance, and the first months of the Peninsular War settled into a costly, squalid conflict. Then in July 1808, the French cause suffered a serious setback. General Pierre Dupont, commanding a corps of French conscripts, found himself surrounded at Bailen in Andalucia by Spanish regulars. To the astonishment of the Spaniards, and the rest of Europe, he surrendered after

scarcely a shot had been fired. This act of cowardice, as Napoleon saw it, sparked panic in the French administration; troops were withdrawn, the Spanish advanced, Joseph quit Madrid, and the French fled northward across the Ebro River.

Napoleon was forced to act to restore French rule, but such a campaign would not be easy. Spain was vast, and the Spanish were elated by their recent victories. Nobody quite knew if the genius of the emperor would be enough to triumph, but all were sure that more was at stake than the crown of Spain.

That November, Napoleon's moves were decisive. French veterans poured across the Ebro, stabbing at the motley Spanish field armies, routing them, and pushing them back. Many of the Spaniards took to their heels or joined bands of guerrillas. Significantly, resistance was collecting at the Aragonese capital of Saragossa, straddling the Ebro. Saragossa had earned a reputation for resoluteness by withstanding the invaders in the summer of 1808 and was now a focal point for the fugitive remnants of armies. After all, if the city could continue to resist the French, Spain might just defeat the master of Europe.

At Tudela on November 23, Marshal Jean Lannes smashed a poorly led Spanish force commanded by General Francisco Castaños, victor of Bailen. Saragossa's garrison was soon joined by survivors from the battle, and they were feverishly impressed into strengthening the city's defenses, overseen by the energetic General José Palafox. Supplies were brought in from the surrounding countryside, troops were reviewed and armed, engineers—overseen by the talented Colonel San Genis, a native of the city—had walls and ditches repaired and houses fortified and loopholed. Barricades were thrown across streets, earthworks were dug, and thousands of sacks filled with earth. The scene was set for one of history's greatest sieges, and Saragossa was readied for a battle to the death.

Marshal Bon Adrien Moncey's III Corps and elements of Marshal Michel Ney's VI Corps, meanwhile, remained around Tudela, catching their breath and awaiting imperial orders. They were not long in coming, and the two marshals and their twenty-five thousand men were soon on the march toward the city. Arriving beneath the walls and setting up camp, they were disconcerted to receive further orders from Napoleon directing Ney to head for Castile, leaving the III Corps alone to defeat the fortified city. Moncey, moreover, had only three of his four divisions at hand, and he flinched from the task of fighting his way into Saragossa. So, to the relief of the Spaniards, the French withdrew, retreating to Alagon to await reinforcements.

A former member of the Spanish Royal Guards, General José Palafox had escaped capture when France deposed the ruling Bourbon monarchy. He returned to his native Aragon and raised an army with which to defend Saragossa.

At the same time, French morale was sagging and a devastated Alagon offered little by way of compensation. A Polish officer in the III Corps, Heinrich von Brandt, recalled: "We camped in conditions of absolute squalor. The inhabitants had fled, the weather was atrocious—freezing northerly gales alternated with torrential downpours without respite."

Reinforcements arrived two weeks later in the form of Marshal Adolphe Mortier's V Corps and the siege train from Bayonne. The bolstered French forces set off again, hoping, perhaps,

that Saragossa would simply capitulate.

Palafox was determined that it would not. He had used the fortnight's respite well, and his garrison boasted thirty-four thousand regular troops and militia, as well as swiftly organized bodies of civilians, many of whom were refugees from the surrounding area. His defense depended upon a series of well-prepared and fortified strongpoints, many of them based on the city's churches, monasteries, and convents. The San José Monastery, just outside the southern wall, acted as a bastion in its own right, as did the Santa Monica Convent, in the southeast of the city, and the Jesús Monastery, on the northern bank of the Ebro just beyond the suburbs. If the French did penetrate into the city, defenders in other substantial buildings—the university, the orphanage, the archbishop's palace, and a score of churches and religious houses—would grind down their advance through the narrow streets and gain time for relief to arrive. There certainly seemed to be sufficient food—at least for the garrison—to endure a three-month siege, and Palafox was sure the garrison possessed the necessary endurance to put up a courageous resistance.

The French began by storming Monte Torrero, an elevated position that dominated the southern side of the city. After just two hours of resistance, the defenders retreated back into the city. That afternoon the understandably optimistic French attacked from the north, with General Honoré Gazan's men bursting into the suburbs. Canister fire from some of the city's 160 guns and ferocious street fighting cost them seven hundred men before they fell back.

Moncey chose this moment to notify Palafox that he should capitulate, but the Spanish commander was scathing, suggesting that the French surrender to him. So General André Lacoste, a talented engineer, began his work in earnest. He determined that in order to effect a breach the French should first seize the San José Monastery, just beyond the shallow Huerba stream. From there the French could reach toward the banks of the Ebro, thus communicating with Gazan, while also launching attacks against the Santa Engracia Gate, thereby gaining access into the south of the city. Trench digging began on December 23, 1808, with shivering conscripts breaking the icy ground and bemoaning their fate and the conditions they were being forced to endure. They were entirely justified, for when, on the twenty-ninth, General Jean Andoche Junot arrived to supercede Moncey, what he found shocked him. He wrote to Napoleon that the III Corps was composed of too few troops to succeed and that its soldiers were "young men, exhausted by the campaign; they are virtually naked, they have no greatcoats and no boots." He continued, "They fill the hospitals…which, due to the poor conditions and the absence of staff, quickly become their tomb." Junot outspokenly informed the emperor that all reports previously sent from Saragossa were tantamount to lies. It was going to be a tough battle with no guarantee of success.

The early days of 1809 saw the French depleted still further when Moncey was ordered to march on Catalayud with General

Soldiers, partisans, and civilian men and women defend a street barricade against a French assault, in an illustration of the Saragossa (Zaragoza in Spanish) siege. Although fanciful, the print accurately depicts the ferocity of the battle for control of the Aragonese city.

Louis Suchet's division, depriving the besiegers of essential manpower. Still, the French were cheered by news of their army's entry into Madrid; Palafox was swift to counter in the propaganda war with a proclamation in which he boasted that he would "sweep this scum away from our walls." Messages from the defenders were even thrown into the French trenches where impressionable conscripts sat shivering. Written in six languages, they tempted the French to desert and join the defense.

But Palafox was being cautious, and his apparent reluctance to risk his troops outside the walls meant that by the second week of January the first of the French siege-battery positions was completed and its guns ready to fire. At 6 A.M. on the tenth, eight French batteries opened up on Saragossa with thirty-two guns, many of them giant twenty-four-pounders, which could hurl a projectile two kilometers. The Spanish suffered heavily from the shot and shell, and their batteries in the San José Monastery were quickly silenced.

The onslaught, however, prompted the first Spanish sortie of note. At midnight a Spanish column raced for the French lines. But the attackers, taken in flank, were scattered and fell back, decimated. The French guns continued to fire, barely interrupted while preparations were made to launch an assault against the San José Monastery. On the afternoon of the eleventh, French officers in the trenches agreed that the breaches blasted in the walls appeared substantial, and that the Spanish seemed suitably cowed by the bombardment. Inside the fort, Mariano Renovales described the fire as being "so intense that hardly a soldier could escape being hit by one projectile or another."

French troops from General Claude Grandjean's division were moved into position, and two light guns were rushed forward to open fire from close range. Three columns of *voltigeurs*, led by Major Stahl, and sappers also charged forward, but were halted by a deep intervening ditch. Fortunately, a captain of the engineers discovered a wooden bridge that the Spaniards had neglected to destroy. He and one hundred hand-picked *voltigeurs* crossed the span and managed to batter their way into the monastery with axes. More French troops were rushed in, and the Spanish 2nd Regiment of Valencia, suffering thirty dead and demoralized by the loss of their colonel, fled in disorder. Renovales reported to Palafox that they had abandoned "a position soaked in blood, covered in arms, legs and torsos."

A few more days of bombardment followed, along with more bloodshed, until the French were confident that an attack on their next target—a Spanish bridgehead on the south side of the Huerba that was protected by a brick wall—was viable. On the evening of the fifteenth, forty Polish *voltigeurs* launched an assault. Through the gloom, a sentry spotted the Poles rushing forward, however, and the alerted Spaniards opened fire and detonated a mine. The attackers emerged through the smoke unharmed and stormed up their ladders and over the wall. Grim bayonet fighting followed before the attackers flushed the defenders out, and the Spanish fled across the Huerba and into the city, burning the bridge behind them.

It was progress for the French, but resistance was still determined. Even so, the city's civilians were suffering enormously. Epidemics were rampant, and rations were much reduced. Shot and shell daily rained down on Saragossa; death and disease stalked the streets. For the besiegers, life that January was almost as grim. The III Corps was reduced to thirteen thousand effectives, and General Gazan had just seven thousand. A January 15 report noted that the 14th Line had 1,812 men under arms and 1,128 in the hospital, the 115th had 1,591 effectives and 1,618 sick, and the Poles of the 1st Vistula Regiment had 1,218 fit and 952 sick. Bands of insurgents, meanwhile, roamed the countryside, attacking French foragers, and supplies dwindled. The dour Colonel Joseph Rogniat of the engineers noted: "Our most terrible enemy, at this time was famine. We lacked meat and our soldiers were reduced to half-rations of bread many times. No village sent in requisitions and the lack of troops since Suchet's division left means that we were not capable of sending sufficiently large detachments out to bring back food."

And all the time Spanish forces were rumored to be on their way to attempt to lift the siege, as indeed they were. General Pedro Elola had gathered two thousand militia and was now advancing in an attempt to break through to Saragossa. News of his army "bringing with it 5,000 muskets" had lifted the spirits of the citizens of Saragossa. The French response was quick: General Pierre Wathier dispersed the insurgents, and Gazan dispatched five hundred soldiers, supported by the 10th Hussars, to prevent them from rallying.

Lacoste, meanwhile, pushed ahead with the placing of new batteries. To frustrate this work, at 4 P.M. on the twenty-first, twenty-four Spanish volunteers under Mariano Galindo sallied forth to attack Battery No. 6. They crossed the Huerba and rushed the guns before being overwhelmed—an act of defiance typical of the besieged Aragonese.

At this critical juncture of the siege, the obstinate and effective Marshal Jean Lannes arrived outside Saragossa to assume overall command of French operations. His presence, coupled with news of a successful action by General Louis Suchet's division of the V Corps—which had scattered armed Spanish peasants and taken up a position to safeguard French communications—raised French morale. Palafox, meanwhile, prepared a Spanish reception for the marshal.

At 4 A.M. on the twenty-third, a single cannon was fired from the Spanish ramparts. Three Spanish battalions "marching in order and silence," according to Lejeune, emerged through the gloomy mist to attack the bleary-eyed defenders of the San José

PRIVATE COLLECTION/BRIDGEMAN ART LIBRARY

On January 22, courageous Marshal Jean Lannes took command of the French army besieging Saragossa. A favorite of Napoleon's, Lannes was mortally wounded later in 1809 at Aspern-Essling, becoming the emperor's first marshal to die as a result of a battle wound.

Shot and shell daily rained down on Saragossa; death and disease stalked the streets. For the besiegers, life that January was almost as grim.

Monastery. The attackers trapped a company of Poles in a house just outside the monastery's walls and set fire to the building, but a French battalion rushed forward and managed to force the Spanish back. While the French were containing the enemy sortie, the Spanish launched a second attack against Battery Nos. 5 and 6. Fifty valiant Spaniards reached the cannons, killed three gunners, and attempted to spike two 12-pounders. A French counterattack, however, swept down upon them, pushed the Spaniards back, recaptured the guns, and took thirty prisoners. The defeat of the sortie prompted Lannes to write to Palafox and declare that his imprudent obstinacy would only result in further casualties. Not receiving a reply, Lannes prepared his men for an all-out assault of the kind the marshal preferred.

The morning of the twenty-sixth was dominated by the monotonous rumble of fifty French guns. Four batteries concentrated on opening a breach in the city wall opposite the San José Monastery, while two strong batteries targeted the Santa Engracia Convent. Despite a thick fog, the city's defenses were battered and pounded for eighteen hours. The Saragossans, as ever, took the punishment, but an additional blow occurred when Colonel San Genis was hit and killed by a round shot.

The following day's grand assault was a French success inasmuch as they fought their way into the city. But the Spanish had lured the French into the maze of Saragossa's streets, where a new style of urban warfare could be waged. As the French attempted to expand their control along Pabostre Avenue onto Del Gato Avenue, they not only met resistance but also came under heavy counterattacks. A fierce assault on the twenty-eighth was beaten off, but at the cost of seventeen men killed and thirty wounded. Rogniat witnessed the attack and noted that "The enemy used a considerable number of grenades and these frightened many of our troops and wounded scores." At 2 P.M. that same day, waves of Spaniards assaulted the French-held Trinitarian Convent. General Claude Rostolland was shot and wounded, and the 117th Line panicked. Only through the exertions of a French captain could a group of grenadiers be rallied and the position saved.

The French continued their methodical advance, and on the twenty-ninth, ninety Poles from the 2nd Vistula Regiment were readied to assault the Santa Monica Convent. Led forward by ten sappers, the Poles were showered with missiles hurled from neighboring houses and forced to scurry for cover. Alternate tactics to an all-out charge were employed. A small explosive charge blasted an opening into a house next to the convent, and French troops quickly poured into the building. From there they broke down a wall and swept into the convent's garden, fighting their way among the cloisters. A force of one hundred grenadiers finally managed to get into the church, wounding General Pedro Villacampa on the way.

Progress was also slow along Santa Engracia Avenue, as each house had to be taken by assault. Sappers under a Major Breuille placed five barrels of powder in the cellar of one house in which defenders were holding out. After blocking the doors and windows, the engineers lit the fuse. The subsequent blast brought down six houses, but as the rubble and dust prevented progress, the sappers determined to use less powder in the future. Charges were henceforth to be just strong enough to blow holes in walls through which assault troops could quickly push.

Elsewhere, 150 Frenchmen defending the Trinitarian Convent faced a particularly brutal attack when a Carmelite monk, San Iago Saas, led hundreds of Spaniards forward through the streets while snipers fanned out on the roofs overlooking the convent. The Spanish attempted to smash down the convent's door with an ax, but sacks of earth placed behind the door prevented the attackers from breaking in. Next the Spaniards brought up a cannon, but the gunners were shot down by the *voltigeurs* of the 15th Line. At 7 P.M. a second, smaller attack followed, but it too failed, leaving a dozen Spaniards sprawled in the street.

The French were not always successful in their own assaults. It was tough going, as Brandt recalled:

We knew that in order not to be killed, or to diminish that risk, we would have to take each and every one of these houses converted into redoubts and where death lurked in the cellars, behind doors and shutters—in fact, everywhere. When we broke into a house we had to make an immediate and thorough inspection from the cellar to the rooftop. Experience taught us that sudden and determined resistance could well be a trick. Often as we were securing one floor we would be shot at from point blank range from the floor above through loopholes in the floorboards. All the nooks and crannies of these old-fashioned houses aided such deadly ambushes. We also had to maintain a good watch on the rooftops. With their light sandals, the Aragonese could move with the ease of and as silently as a cat and were thus able to make surprise incursions well behind the front line. We would be sitting peacefully around a fire, in a house occupied for some days, when suddenly shots would come through some window just as though they had come from the sky itself.

Rogniat confessed in his journal that "The energy with which the enemy defends himself is incredible; the taking of each house necessitates an assault and these fanatics don't only fight from house to house but from floor to floor or from room to room." Lejeune, too, stressed the difficulties encountered by the ordinary soldiers then finding themselves pitted against a determined enemy who contested every pile of rubble. The strain was exhausting the French:

Engineer officers directed the men to spread out along a line and get digging, throwing the earth forward whilst maintaining as much silence as possible otherwise the enemy would shower us with canister. The troops hurry, despite the fatigue brought on by so many nights of such work, hoping to get some rest. And when they sleep even cannon fire can't wake them. But they are not free from danger. There are enemy sorties, bombs, grenades and bullets to fear; the enemy send up shells to illuminate the area and allow marksmen to pick us off. There are stones fired into the air by mortars which come hurtling down, crushing all. Even so the soldiers sleep on perhaps not believing that this sleep might, for them, prove eternal.

Far from being beaten, the Spanish, acting en masse or individually, seemed in their element, keeping the French on their toes, turning the besiegers into the besieged. Those in a supposedly secure area might find themselves ambushed and

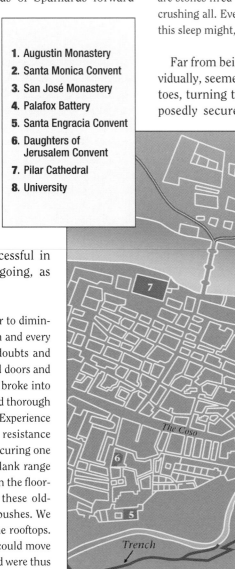

1. Augustin Monastery
2. Santa Monica Convent
3. San José Monastery
4. Palafox Battery
5. Santa Engracia Convent
6. Daughters of Jerusalem Convent
7. Pilar Cathedral
8. University

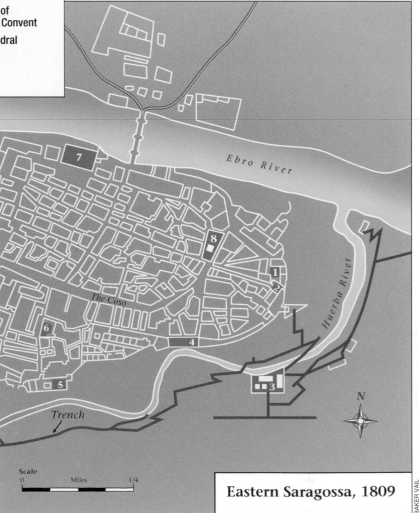

Eastern Saragossa, 1809

forced to watch as their assailants made off over the roofs of the houses. Mines, artillery, snipers all took a terrible toll on both sides, and many questioned how much longer the combatants could persist in this awful battle of attrition.

February began rudely when at 5 in the morning on the first the French detonated a mine under the San Augustin Monastery. Grenadiers of the 44th Line surprised and flushed out the dazed garrison. The Spanish recovered quickly and counterattacked, and a deadly battle flared up around the altar. French reserves were rushed in and tipped the battle in France's favor. A few Spanish defenders who found themselves trapped in the bell tower made the most of their situation by throwing grenades down on the French. A large second counterattack freed the trapped men.

General Lacoste also was mortally wounded on February 1. Lejeune saw it happen and recounted:

Lacoste had told me to detonate my mines two minutes after I heard his mines go off. When the moment came we lit the fuse and ten or a dozen houses were blown into the air followed by a deep boom. It took

> ## 'We lit the fuse and ten or a dozen houses were blown into the air followed by a deep boom.'

some time for the dust to settle but no sooner had it than Prost ran forward followed by the Polish assault party. Lacoste and Valaze arrived just as they went into the attack and we all clambered up onto the ruins of a house in order to get a better view. We cheered on the Poles but our shouts attracted attention from the Spanish hiding behind walls and peeking through gaps and holes. They opened fire hitting Lalobe and General Lacoste; the former died instantly but Lacoste followed him a few hours later.

Colonel Rogniat assumed command of the engineers, but he was wounded in the hand the following day.

The French continued to grind through the city, advancing around Pabostre and even occupying some houses on Quemada Avenue, but the attackers failed to properly secure these positions. Ever watchful for an opportunity, the Spaniards launched an attack that swept the French right back into Pabostre. Palafox was quick to proclaim a victory, but the next day the French were back in rubble-strewn Quemada Avenue and pushing toward the Hospital of the

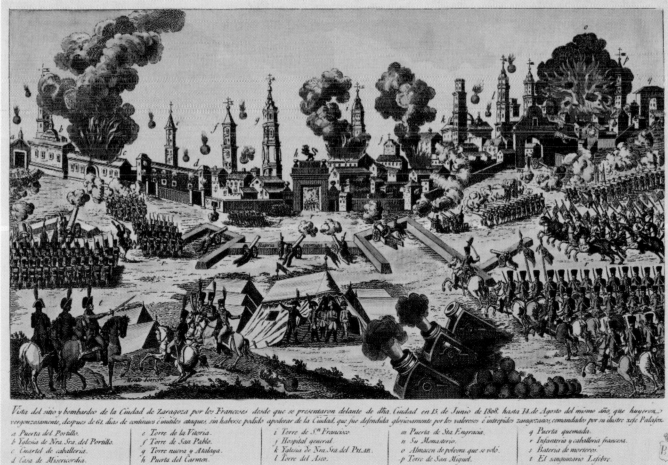

ARCHIVO ICONGRAFICO, S.A./CORBIS

Flaming shells fall on Saragossa during the French army's first siege of the city, from June to August 1808. That unsuccessful operation concentrated on breaking into the city from the south, whereas the second siege, which began on December 20, pierced its eastern defenses.

Orphans. There they met more determined resistance. A Lieutenant Brenne, leading one attack, was wounded three times before his troops were finally repelled. An attack against the Daughters of Jerusalem Convent was also attempted. Breaking into the building, French *voltigeurs* were floored by Spanish musket fire coming from behind a loopholed wall. Working their way round, they outflanked the position and secured the convent.

French sappers, using mines charged with five hundred pounds of powder, successfully blasted their way along Oleta Avenue, and for the first time the besieging army reached the city's main thoroughfare—the Coso, which runs the length of Saragossa. But by that point most French troops were securing overrun enclaves within the city; too few could be spared for more offensive operations. Lannes hastily instructed Gazan to apply pressure against the portion of Saragossa on the Ebro's northern bank, but that general's first attempt ended badly. Climbing out of trenches filled with ankle-deep, freezing water, the French rushed forward but were picked off by Spanish marksmen on the roof of the Jesús Convent.

Lannes thereafter did what he could to maintain the French momentum, switching assaults from one quarter to another,

> **'A neighboring** house collapsed and unmasked a Spanish battery which blasted us with grape at point blank range.'

keeping the Aragonese stretched and under fire. Nevertheless, it was proving difficult to secure a solid foothold on the Coso, let alone move beyond it. Brandt recalled the scene:

Our entire division took part in the assault on the Coso. Above the continual bickering of musketry the groans of much larger explosions could be heard— sometimes the booming of cannon and sometimes a mine going off. I was busy in the Coso with a detachment of some fifty men, setting up a barricade. Grenadiers, posted above us in the windows of neighboring houses, covered this work, which was designed to protect a communications trench which ran from one side of the street to the other. Suddenly our ears were almost shattered by the familiar whistling and roaring noise of an exploding mine. A neighboring house collapsed and unmasked a Spanish battery which blasted us with grape at point blank range. Miraculously, only three men were hit but the rest ran for it as quick as they could.

Gazan was not deterred by his initial repulse and continued to launch attack after attack. Lejeune witnessed the decisive one: "200 grenadiers and 300 *voltigeurs* throw themselves forward in a number of columns and break into the Jesús Convent. 400 Spaniards, demoralized by the bombardment, do not wait

Eugene Lucas y Padilla's painting The Siege of Saragossa *focuses on the terrible plight of the city's civilians. Saragossa's prewar population of sixty thousand was swelled by an influx of refugees, fighters, and laborers prior to the second French siege. By the time the city surrendered, the fierce battle had claimed the lives of an estimated thirty thousand civilians and left tens of thousands homeless.*

to defend themselves. They turn tail and we seize control." It was an all too unusual success. Mostly, French officers such as Rogniat were convinced that "the only way to defeat such obstinate defenders is to kill them." Want and disease were doing part of the job for them. Some five hundred inhabitants were dying daily; many of their bodies lay unburied in the streets. Survivors, meanwhile, cowered in cellars or fought back against the French. Shells rained down, igniting fires among the city's ruined buildings; smoke shrouded the infernal scene. And slowly, ever so slowly, the French increased their control over the city.

A mine of unprecedented size—three thousand pounds—was carefully placed under the San Francisco Monastery. The fuses were lit, and Lejeune was there to see the explosion and watch the subsequent French assault:

Brave Colonel Dupeyroux with his regiment and Valaze and his engineers were waiting in the ruins of the hospital for the signal. Breuille detonated the mine and it blew in part of the convent's walls. The bell-tower, which we had expected to see collapse, remained standing. Although the dust still billowed in choking clouds Valaze and his troops swept into the building, flushing out the defenders with the bayonet. The assault was so brilliant that Palafox called the entire garrison to arms, fearing that we would break into the very centre of the city. We had hoped that Spanish resistance would collapse with shock but our attack seemed instead to rather provoke their ire.

Despite the blast, the fighting in the church was bitter. Intermingled Spaniards and French savagely fought their way down the nave and up the stairs of the bell tower. Refusing to surrender, Spanish defenders were hurled to their deaths.

French success stirred alarm across the city; the tocsins dolefully sounded, drums were beaten, and every available Spaniard was mustered in the central marketplace. Palafox hesitated to launch an attack; instead he issued a proclamation in which, among other things, he promised to hunt down defeatists and declared that "our friends in America" were "preparing enormous sums for the repair" of the city's war-ravaged buildings. The San Francisco Monastery, for one, had been completely wrecked. According to Baron Lejeune:

The explosion had not only destroyed a large part of the building but also many of the cellars in which families had been sheltering in order to avoid the bombardment; in addition more than 400 defenders, including an entire company of grenadiers from the Regiment of Valencia, had been blown to smithereens. The gardens and the surrounding land were a horror to behold, strewn with masses of human remains. It was impossible to make a step without standing on something.

The Maid of Saragossa

During the first siege of the city, a young woman named Augustina was taking provisions to artillerymen when she approached a shaken gun crew. According to legend, she grabbed a linstock from a gunner and touched it to the nearby cannon (above). As soon as the gun had discharged, she sprang onto it and vowed not to leave the cannon while she was still alive, thereby inspiring the Spanish defenders and becoming known as the "Maid of Saragossa." She continued to serve as a gunner in the second siege. Her tale moved Lord Byron to write of her in his poem *Childe Harold's Pilgrimage*.

On February 12, the destructive fighting reached Saragossa's university. Brandt recalled that "the first attack on the university buildings failed due to the fact that the miners had not been able to place their galleries close enough under the walls, the result being that the explosion failed to make a breach and our columns were exposed to a galling fire from which they fell back with the loss of about forty men."

Recovering quickly, the French brought up a twelve-pounder along with a mortar to blast an opening, but the officer directing the guns was picked off by a sniper. When the cannons finally opened fire, the defenders responded by plugging gabions and sandbags into the widening breach, making it impossible for the French infantry to charge through.

Such tenacious resistance in part stemmed from despair, but also from rumors that a large relief force had gathered at Lerida, about eighty miles to the southeast. In fact, some twelve thousand Spanish troops were on the march, and Lannes was forced to take some of Gazan's men and march north to defeat the attempt to relieve Saragossa. For many in the garrison, it seemed one promise too many. On February 14 an entire company of Swiss mercenaries fighting for the Spanish deserted to the French. More drama followed when one hundred desperate citizens broke out of the city and approached the French lines, asking to be taken prisoner. The French commanders cleverly turned this to their advantage. They gave the civilians bread and sent them back into Saragossa to spread the word that the French would treat the citizens honorably and, more important, feed them.

Spanish morale deteriorated further when the promised relief did not arrive. On February 16, Lannes received a letter from Paris promising everything he might need to complete the siege: reinforcements, supplies, soldiers' pay for January, and surgeons. The scales, it seemed, were slowly swinging in France's favor.

Still the defenders fought back, contesting every house, every garden. A particular problem for the French was sniper fire, and artillery and engineer officers were favorite targets. On February 17, Lannes, having driven off the Spanish field army, returned to Saragossa and was almost hit by a sniper's musket ball. Furious, he climbed the bell tower of the Jesús Convent, had fifteen loaded muskets brought up, and began trying to pick off the enemy marksman. But the French marshal was soon targeted by a Spanish cannon, a round shot from which killed a captain standing next to him.

At 8 A.M. the next day—seemingly in retaliation—the French unleashed a massive bombardment; fifty-two guns pulverized the archbishop's palace and cathedral. Gazan launched three columns of troops in an attack against defenders in the shattered Lazarus Monastery. Two columns were repulsed, but the third broke into the monastery's church and pressed on toward the bridge over the swift-running Ebro River. The dramatic attack cut off a considerable number of Spaniards on the northern bank. While some three hundred forced their way over the bridge and others fled across the river in boats, some twenty-five hundred Spaniards became French prisoners. Lannes' engineers capitalized on the successful assault by quickly barring and fortifying the entrance to the bridge.

Just as the Spanish were surrendering on the northern bank, a massive detonation was heard from the center of the city. Having made a series of attacks and determined that the buildings were packed with defenders, the French had detonated a fifteen-hundred-pound mine planted in the cellar of the university's main building. The defenders were so dazed by the ensuing explosion, which blew a large hole in the building's outer wall, that Polish and French attackers not only broke into the gutted compound but were able to push on as far as the Trinity Church. The next morning, the French detonated a mine under that sacred building, occupied it, and captured two guns.

The French advances formed a deep wedge in the Spanish position, and Palafox, then seriously ill, believed he could do little to reverse the situation. No relief force would be forthcoming; nothing more could be done. The Spanish general finally sent one of his aides to Lannes to ask for a cease-fire. The French commander rejected the proposal and, to underline his words, positioned a powerful battery close by the bridge over the Ebro. Palafox's response was to resign, leaving his command to a junta of forty notables, who deliberated throughout the night to the tune of detonating mines.

Fearing a public backlash, and hardly daring to whisper the word surrender, the junta was divided. Epidemics were claiming the lives of five hundred people a day. The French were stubbornly, if slowly, plowing their way through the rubble, their noose becoming tighter and tighter. The forty Spaniards summoned up the courage—for it took courage to surrender after such a siege—to dispatch a second messenger to Lannes, asking for a suspension of hostilities. At 4 P.M. the marshal ordered the artillery to stop firing and sent an officer into the city demanding surrender within two hours. Lannes revealed that he had prepared six three-thousand-pound mines beneath the Coso. The junta bowed its head to the inevitable and accepted Lannes' terms.

A Spanish priest wields a crucifix as French troops charge one of the city's fortresslike churches. Local clerics played a conspicuous role during the siege, and after Saragossa's surrender, the French executed a number of them for inciting resistance.

corpses, heaps of ashes, and rubble. Makeshift hospitals were clogged with the dead and dying, as were cellars and houses—anyplace, in fact, where the populace had attempted to shelter from the 32,700 shells and round shot fired into the city. The central marketplace resembled a cemetery, the cathedral a charnel house. The French army camped outside the city for fear of epidemics. Lannes had lost three thousand dead and fifteen thousand wounded, most of whom were dying. Heavy casualties, but virtually nothing compared to that of the Spaniards—a staggering 53,873 dead, according to the city authorities.

Aragon's capital had undergone a holocaust quite unlike anything it had ever endured—a siege "extraordinary and terrible," according to Rogniat. Nothing quite like it would be seen until Stalingrad. The city's surrender seemed to break resistance in Aragon, and four years of French occupation followed. But to the rest of Spain the example of Saragossa was inspirational, and Spaniards recalled the siege with immense pride. Outside of Spain, Saragossa earned the country almost universal praise, and not only from those countries at war, or soon to be at war, with France. Europe caught its breath that February, as French power had been stretched to its limit by one gallant city.

Although Spanish courage at Saragossa would be widely celebrated, the siege had been a heroic feat for the French as well. Lejeune wrote that thirteen thousand men had braved hunger, fatigue, and danger to force one hundred thousand citizens to capitulate. But the victory came at a terrible cost in morale. The French had outwardly laughed off Spanish resistance and fanaticism, but their martial confidence was shaken to its core by the siege of Saragossa. How could they, the liberators of Europe, be so despised as to provoke such resistance? How many more Saragossas would be needed to pacify such a country? Questions such as these weighed heavily on the hitherto enthusiastic soldiers of Napoleon's empire. There could be no glory for them in Spain.

Far away in Paris, Napoleon heard of the surrender on the twenty-seventh of February, but he had already turned his back on the peninsula and was planning to march his legions against Austria. He, for one, would not be returning to Spain but would leave it to his generals to find what glory they could in war-torn Iberia.

T he day of glory, if such it could be called, was long in coming. On the morning of Tuesday, February 21, 1809, the Spanish garrison marched out of the Portillo Gate and piled its arms before marching off into captivity. According to Brandt, it was a motley army:

After about an hour, the vanguard of the famous defenders of Saragossa began to appear. Not long after we witnessed the arrival of the rest of the army: a strange collection composed of humanity of all shades and conditions. A few were in uniform but most were dressed like peasants….Most of them were of such non-military bearing that our men were saying aloud that we should never have had so much trouble in beating such a rabble.

They numbered only eighty-five hundred (a few thousand more were flushed out from hiding in the next few days). The city was a horror to behold. Its narrow streets were choked with

JONATHAN NORTH translated and edited Heinrich von Brandt's recollections of his service in the French army, *In the Legions of Napoleon: The Memoirs of a Polish Officer in Spain and Russia 1808-1813* (Greenhill Books, 1999).

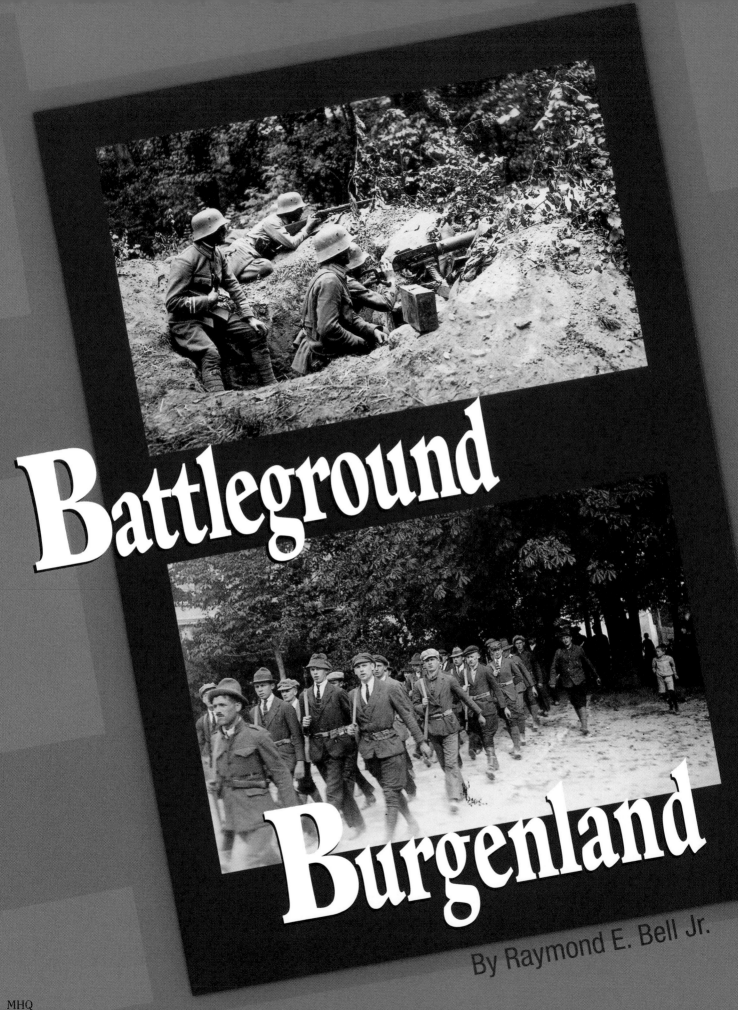

Battleground

Burgenland

By Raymond E. Bell Jr.

Shortly after World War I, a border war for possession of the traditionally Hungarian province of Burgenland became a test for Austria's new, leftist army.

On the fifth of September 1921, Franz Samotny, an army private and member of the Austrian Communist Party, died for his country. A soldier in the newly organized Austrian army's 2nd Battalion, 5th Infantry Regiment, he was killed in battle against right-wing Hungarian guerrillas on the outskirts of the small Austrian border town of Kirchschlag. The clash there was one of the most significant small-unit actions fought in the armed struggle between the left-leaning Austrian government and the rightist Hungarian monarchy, headed by its regent, Admiral Miklos Horthy. At issue was possession of the province known as Burgenland. The outcome of the dispute was that Burgenland became a battleground. What is uncanny is that these events, which transpired in the early 1920s, bear an eerie resemblance to events that recently took place in the nearby Balkans.

Franz Samotny's participation in the action on the outskirts of Kirchschlag was the result of a festering international situation brought about by the breakup in 1918 of the Austro-Hungarian empire. Allied with Germany in World War I, the heterogeneous empire disintegrated with the defeat of the Central Powers. Fragments of the former multinational realm soon found themselves at war with one another. One of the more controversial situations was Burgenland's status with regard to the new states of Austria and Hungary.

The postwar Treaty of St. Germain-en-Laye reduced Austrian territory to the country's German-speaking areas (Italy, however, was given the German-speaking Tyrol), and Hungary lost three-quarters of its prewar territory under terms of the Treaty of Trianon. The Austro-Hungarian border delineated in the treaties placed Burgenland in Austria. Most of the province was German speaking, and its inhabitants showed a strong inclination to be a part of Austria. Nevertheless, Hungarians, even as they were struggling with ethnic minorities along other borders, claimed Burgenland as their own. Under the empire, the province had been part of Hungary, and during the regency of Admiral Horthy, the country launched a campaign to convince Burgenlanders to become citi-

Above left: Austrian soldiers man a machine gun position at the border of the contested province of Burgenland in September 1921. Below left: Hungarian "irregulars" display suspiciously military discipline as they march through Burgenland. Right: A pro-Austrian political poster urges the populace of Ödenburg to "Trust not the flattering tunes! Stay German!"

zens of the "new" Hungary. The propaganda onslaught produced a period of great instability not only in Burgenland but also along the eastern borders of the recognized Austrian provinces of Lower Austria, Styria, and Vienna.

Burgenland had strategic geopolitical significance for both Austria and Hungary. The province's northwest border just skirted the suburbs of the city-province of Vienna, the capital of Austria. If Burgenland became a Hungarian province, it would mean that Austria's major metropolitan area would be located hard on Hungary's western border. Horthy was an ultraconservative who in 1920 had driven from power a Hungarian Communist regime. Because Vienna was a stronghold of the leftist Social Democrats, then a major power in Austrian politics, the juxtaposition of right-wing Hungary to a strong left-wing nation's capital could easily lead to trouble. Indeed, the Communists in Austria still participated in the political process, and many party adherents, such as Franz Samotny, served in the army.

To complicate matters further, the Austrian army in 1921 was a bone of contention between right and left political elements within the country itself, and many citizens had grave doubts about its quality. Rightists saw the new force as potentially ineffective because of the large number of Social Democratic soldiers in the organization. Those on the left, on the other hand, saw the soldiers as patriots dedicated to preserving a democratic state.

The army's size was dictated by the Treaty of St. Germain-en-Laye. It limited the military establishment to an authorized strength of thirty thousand officers, noncommissioned officers, and men—hardly greater than a large city police force. In addition, the army could have no large-caliber artillery, tanks, aircraft, or chemical weapons. The treaty terms were so restrictive that they even specified the maximum number of machine guns with which a unit could be equipped.

The terms, however, did allow one choice. The Austrians could opt for organizing either divisions or smaller, mixed brigades. According

to the treaty, the brigades would include infantry, bicycle troops, cavalry, artillery, and mortars—about five thousand men altogether. The government decided to organize six combined-arms brigades. The population of a particular province determined the size of the contingent stationed within its borders. Vienna, for example, had a garrison consisting of almost one-third of the army, while the small, far-west province of Vorarlberg had a contingent of only six hundred. This small, simply equipped, and untried army eventually settled the issue of to which country—Hungary or Austria—Burgenland would belong.

The Austrians' adversaries were irregular forces covertly supported by the Hungarian government. Hungary's strategy to acquire Burgenland was for the people of the province, after "persuasion" by insurgents, to declare their independence from Austria. Regular Hungarian military and paramilitary organizations were initially withdrawn from the region and replaced by guerrilla organizations. These irregulars were recruited from all over Hungary except the province of "West Hungary" (Burgenland).

The U.S. military attaché to Austria summed up the Hungarian strategy

Burgenland in 1921

 August Clashes
 September Clashes
 November Clashes

BAKER VAIL

when he reported to Washington that the insurgents were not only to defend the territory to be annexed but also to drive Austrian influence out of the region. They would next invade Austria proper and through their presence oblige the Austrian government to abandon all claim to Burgenland in perpetuity. Finally, in light of the authoritarian Hungarian regime's philosophical opposition to the socialist Austrian state, an important goal was to provoke a revolt or coup by Austrian reactionaries.

To officially disassociate itself from covert operations, Hungary allowed recruiting to proceed clandestinely. It established a recruiting bureau in Budapest that ostensibly was an employment agency for a charitable institution. In addition, organizers sought men, especially students or the unemployed, for membership in an association known as the Free Lancer Corps. They were offered one hundred Hungarian *Kronen* per day plus food, clothing, and tobacco. An added incentive was the promise of unlimited plunder.

In order to disguise the Hungarian effort even further, the government concocted a rather simplistic deception. The police occasionally arrested members of the Free Lancer Corps on trumped-up charges. After due publicity had been given to the arrests and supposed punishment, the alleged perpetrators were then quietly released from custody.

The Hungarian government proceeded rapidly from recruitment to organizing the insurgents into units. The company became the basic combat formation. Each company was to consist of five officers and 250 enlisted men. The unit was authorized ten machine guns but only fifty hand grenades. Hungarian plans called for raising a force of some thirty thousand men.

The Austrian army was originally not supposed to become involved in the Burgenland issue. The Allied Military Control Commission, which was supervising the permanent accession of Burgenland to Austria, did not want the army participating in what it considered a police matter. Instead, Austrian gendarmes, border guards, and customs officials were to establish a presence in the province. Small groups of these men were to move to their respective locations on August 28, 1921, and be ready to assume their duties the following day.

But matters did not go as planned. On marching into Burgenland, the gendarmerie was almost immediately attacked by Hungarian guerrilla bands. Several gendarmes were mortally wounded or taken prisoner during fight-

The Hungarians not only disarmed the policemen but stripped them of their uniforms and generally mistreated them.

many others taken prisoner. Yet the Austrian paramilitary forces were not willing to completely abandon their efforts to make their presence felt, and many of the embattled policemen continued to man their posts.

In the meantime, the Austrian army had not remained idle. When in early summer intelligence sources had indicated that Hungary was doing what it could to actively support an insurgency in Burgenland, the Austrian Ministry for Military Affairs placed a number of army

Hungarian insurgents lead Austrian gendarmes captured at Au am Leithagebirge through the city of Eisenstadt on September 28, 1921. In 1925, Eisenstadt became Burgenland's provincial capital.

ing with insurgents around the villages of Siggendorf and St. Margerethen in the northern and central parts of Burgenland. Similar clashes in other parts of the province yielded equally unsettling results. Commission representatives in Ödenburg responded by recommending that the gendarmes halt their deployments in the province.

But that recommendation only encouraged the Hungarians to step up their attacks, and the insurgents launched a series of sudden onslaughts against the lightly protected gendarmerie posts. On August 31, for in-

stance, the guerrillas captured seventeen Austrian gendarmes and took them to the town of St. Gotthard in Hungary. Apparently to intimidate the Austrian government and its paramilitary forces, the Hungarians not only disarmed the policemen but stripped them of their uniforms and generally mistreated them. By September 8, realizing that the gendarmerie could not assume their duties, the Allied Military Control Commission recommended that the policemen be withdrawn from Burgenland.

By that time, thirteen Austrians had been killed, thirty-two wounded, and

units on alert. The orders to be prepared to deploy to predesignated defensive positions, if need be, were issued to infantry units as well as cavalry and engineers. Then, as the gendarmerie, customs officials, and border guards began their late-August advance, army units began to deploy along Lower Austria's border with Burgenland.

By August 31, with news of the gendarmes' difficulties having reached Vienna, army troops were in positions along the border. The next day, units alerted in the Austrian province of Styria deployed to that province's boundary with Burgen-

land. In all, seven infantry battalions of about six hundred men each and two one-hundred-man cavalry squadrons took up defensive positions to prevent any incursion into sovereign Austrian territory. Additional infantry, artillery, and engineer units throughout Austria were also put on alert status.

The deployments had a significance for the army above and beyond that of responding to an incipient national emergency. At their home stations, the soldiers were subjected to insults about their membership in an allegedly incompetent and worthless organization—the new Austrian army. The verbal attacks had begun to cause resentment and indignation among the army's ranks just as the soldiers were starting to consider themselves professionals. The escalating situation in Burgenland, however, could provide the Austrian military force with an opportunity to eliminate any doubt as to its competency.

The soldiers were nevertheless supported by a wave of patriotism that swept across the country. Many Austrians viewed the Burgenland border affair as a threat to the entire country. If the confrontation intensified, the army might well have to fight. That the government of Hungary was considered reactionary also was not lost on an Austrian army predominantly composed of soldiers belonging to a military labor union. Moreover, many of the troops had a strong socialist bent.

The Hungarian insurgents, meanwhile, had an almost indefinite amount of time to disrupt the formal takeover of Burgen-

land by the Austrians. Those directing insurgent operations prepared to carry their struggle for the province into Austria itself. They believed such a strategy would isolate Burgenland from Austria proper and convince the province's inhabitants that only Hungary could provide them security. It was therefore allegedly in the people's interests to become Hungarian citizens. The strategy also would prevent the Austrian government from exerting control in Burgenland and from influencing any self-determination measures the Austrian-leaning Burgenlanders might take. Hungarians reasoned that attacks on Austrian border towns would also force Austria's military onto the defensive and divert the public's attention from Burgenland to the army's struggle to justify its very existence.

Using this strategy as guidance, militant Hungarians began to plan a series of attacks on border villages and towns with the primary aim of psychologically intimidating the Burgenland population. The Hungarian government had approved the plans, which called for its full support in providing supplies, protecting caches of weapons, and establishing safe havens for insurgent activities. At the same time, authorities implemented cover plans for masking official approval of guerrilla operations.

In addition to recruiting through front organizations, the Hungarian government set up well-stocked supply depots in Ocedenbürg and Oberwarth. Secure locations throughout the country for storing weapons and equipment supplemented the logistical nodes. The

Hungarian army made large quantities of arms, ammunition, and military accouterments available. Although the insurgents generally wore civilian clothes, they were equipped with army helmets. Each guerrilla was issued belts capable of holding 120 rounds of ammunition. The most overt official Hungarian participation in the campaign, however, was the medical support provided by regular Hungarian army soldiers.

Insurgents began operations by threatening and harassing key influential individuals in Burgenland. Physical and psychological abuse was heaped on village elders, teachers, and public officials. Simultaneously the insurgents developed detailed plans for launching attacks on border towns and hamlets.

The guerrillas found support among the Hungarian landowners in the province, who had the most to gain from Burgenland becoming a permanent part of Hungary instead of part of socialist-leaning Austria. As a result, the landowners not only willingly cooperated with the insurgents but also provided the necessary accommodations for their caches of supplies, equipment, ammunition, and weapons.

Most Burgenlanders, however, were either ambivalent toward the Hungarian cause or supported union with Austria. Those favoring the latter, when they could be identified, became targets of intimidation along with individuals who had influence. The guerrillas actually did little to win support for the Hungarian cause. Instead of posing as protectors of the Burgenlanders, the insurgents wantonly went about coercing the population into providing money, food, and supplies for their bands. These forced "contributions" ultimately turned even the most ambivalent Burgenlander against any idea of becoming a Hungarian citizen.

The coercive behavior of the guerrillas, moreover, established a favorable environment for the eventual introduc-

tion of Austrian army units. It became more and more apparent that Austrian military action was necessary to prevent the intimidation of the populace and the attacks on Austrian gendarmes and other government officials. Austrian military commanders now began to defend the border and take over the occupation mission originally assigned to paramilitary forces.

Austrian Brig. Gen. Rudolf Vidossich, who was appointed director of military operations in Burgenland, had overseen the first step: the deployment of troops to positions along the provincial borders of Vienna, Styria, and Lower Austria. Although General Vidossich had been an officer in the Austro-Hungarian army, he had managed to win the trust of a Social Democratic government leadership suspicious of high-ranking officers of the former conservative regime.

While the army units deployed, the government in Vienna developed two sets of plans. The first directed how Austria's established borders were to be defended. The second dealt with the occupation of Burgenland. The first set assumed possible combat. The second authorized a show of force, but was to be as peaceful as possible.

The defense plans called for establish-ing strongpoints in border towns and on important terrain features. The army identified a set of likely targets of insurgent attacks and dispatched troops to set up appropriate positions to defend those vulnerable locales. The major rail link between Austria and Hungary, for example, went through the Austrian border town of Bruck, on the Leitha River and in the province of Vienna. A company of approximately one hundred soldiers of the 3rd Battalion, 1st Infantry Regiment, defended this key location.

The nature of the Burgenland terrain also influenced the defense plans. The hilly topography of much of the province allowed for good defensive positions. On the other hand, a force approaching an Austrian position could often take advantage of the cover and concealment that some terrain afforded attackers.

The distance over which Austrian defense forces had to operate was also an important consideration. There were not enough soldiers for an effective cordon along the entire border, and the gaps between army units were too great for bicycle troops and cavalry to respond quickly to hit-and-run attacks.

Establishing strongpoints and adopting aggressive patrolling tactics were determined to be the most effective way to overcome terrain disadvantages. Communications units' radios and wire equipment, supplemented with the liberal use of commercial telephone lines, linked the strongpoints. The army conducted combat patrols principally on foot and horseback in rough and wooded terrain, and on bicycle and by motor vehicle on the flatland. Small units would move from strongpoint to strongpoint at irregular intervals in an attempt to intercept and disrupt insurgent activity. Such defensive tactics tended to destroy the enemy's ability to choose the best time and place to attack.

To strengthen the border, searchlights illuminated routes the enemy was likely to take at night, a favorite striking time for the guerrillas. Taking advantage of their artillery's range, Austrians set up batteries to cover areas they could not cover with small-arms, mortar, and machine gun fire. This integration of different army tactics, equipment, and weaponry was ahead of its time and proved to be the most effective use of the military's assets in a defensive role.

The Austrian army's occupation plans for Burgenland took an entirely different tack. When, and if, the time came to enter Burgenland, plans called for a two-phase advance. The first would be made in the northern part of the province. If it was successful, a second, southern phase would be executed. The plan had several advantages, although at first glance it appears to have been somewhat timid. First, the small Austrian army would not be biting off more than it could chew at one time. Second, from a logistical perspective, the plan took into account how best to supply the advancing troops. The road network and proximity of the action to Vienna, where most of the supplies would originate, favored a sequential occupation. Once the northern area was secured, forward supply bases could be established in newly liberated locations to service the next phase. A third advantage was that before the second phase was launched, the effectiveness of the first part could be assessed and, if necessary, corrections made to the plan. Successful completion of both phases would signal the capability of the new Austrian army. At the same time, it would encourage the growing confidence of the Austrian soldiers in their own prowess.

The occupation plan, nevertheless, carried special risks for the Austrian government. It gave Hungarian authorities more time to consolidate their hold in the south, especially around and in Ödenburg, a town strongly disposed toward Hungary. The Hungarian government could then change its policy from intimi-dating the people to one that would make Hungarian citizenship more attractive to Burgenlanders. If the guerrillas could defeat the first phase of the Austrian plan, the southern part of Burgenland could conceivably fall to Hungary with a minimum of effort.

So the stage was set for making Burgenland and the border towns a battleground upon which the Austrian army could prove itself and the Hungarian covert forces could deny Austrian citizenship to Burgenlanders. By the time the army had completed its September 1 move to the Burgenland border, fighting had already broken out between Austrian soldiers and Hungarian insurgents.

On August 31, guerrillas struck the small town of Hohenbrugg, just inside Styria and west of St. Gotthard. Hohenbrugg lay on a major route from Hungary into Austria, which facilitated the

insurgents' attack and withdrawal. Because the town was also in the southern-most part of the Burgenland, it was harder for the Austrians to supply and reinforce their forces there. Although St. Gotthard was a good base for insurgent operations, newly arrived Austrian units drove off the guerrillas without suffering any casualties.

Hohenbrugg, however, continued to prove a tempting target, and guerrillas struck there again on September 3. That same day they attacked the town of Sinnersdorf, on the Styria-Burgenland border near the Pinka River and nestled in the foothills of the Fischbacher Alps.

Hungarian irregulars issue permits to civilians in Mattersdorf in an attempt to exercise political control, in October 1921. In 1925 the town was renamed Mattersburg.

Relatively isolated in the northeastern corner of Styria, the town offered a good target for a swift attack. The fact that Austrian troops assigned to the defense of the border were just arriving worked to the insurgents' advantage. But as at Hohenbrugg, the Austrian troops again defeated their attackers without suffering any losses.

Then on September 5, Franz Samotny was mortally wounded during the battle for Kirchschlag. In attacking the popular resort town, Hungarians hoped to make a political as well as a military statement. Communications with the largest nearby Austrian city of Wiener Neustadt were tenuous, and the limited road network complicated reinforcing the troops at Kirchschlag. An advantage for the Hungarians was that they could count on support from sympathizers in nearby Ödenburg. Kirchschlag itself had no political or strategic military value,

but because the town was visited by many people from elsewhere in Austria during the ongoing vacation season, a successful Hungarian insurgent attack there would have considerable psychological value. If the army failed to defeat the insurgents, the tourists could be expected to spread word about the terror precipitated by guerrilla action as well as criticism of the ineffectiveness of the Austrian forces. The attacks of the previous few days had been of a limited nature. The battle of Kirchschlag would be the first real opportunity for the new army to prove itself. The town's garrison, the 2nd Battalion, 5th Infantry, was composed primarily of soldiers from socialist Vienna. Their performance would be watched carefully by the army's leftist supporters and rightist detractors.

Early in the morning on September 5, soldiers positioned just to the east of Kirchschlag along the road to Pilgersdorf, in Burgenland, heard a large volume of gunfire from the direction of the latter town. The alerted soldiers waited apprehensively for word of what was happening. Soon a detachment of forty men of the gendarmerie and finance security posts near Pilgersdorf came streaming down the road toward Kirchschlag in great disorder. They excitedly told the soldiers that they had been driven from their posts and were being pursued by armed Hungarians. As the Austrian paramilitary officials stumbled into town, their disheveled appearance and confused speech spread panic among both locals and vacationers, and many prepared to flee into the neighboring hills.

The senior Austrian commander in town, Colonel Emil Sommer, quickly dispatched Captain Alexander Dini with a platoon of soldiers to investigate. In the meantime, Sommer posted his two heavy machine guns on heights to the east of town to cover the approaches from Burgenland.

Dini's unit advanced cautiously eastward as he tried to determine the location and strength of what he correctly assumed was a band of guerrillas. As the soldiers were advancing through the heavy woods along either side of the road, the insurgents suddenly opened fire on them with rifles and machine guns. Dini's men had run into a force of some three hundred guerrillas, who pursued them closely as they retreated toward Kirchschlag.

Colonel Sommer's men, meanwhile, were manning forward positions outside of the town. Dini's retreating soldiers passed through the Austrian lines in good order and took up their prearranged fighting positions. As the insurgents came within range, Sommer ordered his riflemen and machine-gunners to open fire. The fusillade from the well-positioned soldiers stopped the charging guerrillas cold. Withering under the concentrated Austrian fire, the Hungarians simply melted back into the countryside, leaving twenty-one bodies behind.

The cost to the Austrians was five men killed, fourteen wounded, and three taken prisoner. The losses represented about 9 percent of the battalion's strength, which meant that the Hungarians, with an estimated strength of three hundred, outnumbered the Austrians approximately 2-to-1. The relatively small strength of the 2nd Battalion—not all of them present at Kirchschlag—shows how thinly stretched the army was along the border. More important, however, was the fact that an Austrian army unit of significant size had demonstrated it could perform adequately in the face of the enemy.

Aside from being a successful baptism of fire, the action had other significance. Up until the clash there had been no clear connection between the insurgents and the Hungarian armed forces. Officially the insurgents were local patriots fighting to free their province from Austrian domination. Evidence discovered on one of the guerrilla's bodies, however, told a different story. The Austrians found the uniform of a Hungarian army lieutenant and a matriculation certificate to Budapest University inside the man's knapsack. An Austrian newspaper

concluded, not surprisingly, that the dead man was a Hungarian army officer in disguise.

The short battle for Kirchschlag was especially noteworthy for its brutality. Three prisoners captured by the Hungarians were tortured and murdered. Private Ferdinand Käemper was one of the prisoners. The insurgents stripped him, tied his hands behind his back, bayoneted him repeatedly, and hung him with telephone wire from an apple tree. Such treatment of prisoners was not limited to combatants. Austrian medical aide Hugo Mladenka was bayoneted as he lay defenseless on the ground. The

Late in the conflict some Hungarians dropped the pretense of their nonmilitary status. Count Tamas Erdödy (third from left) posed with his unit in uniform—as did his wife.

perpetrator, in turn, fell victim to an Austrian sharpshooter's bullet. The fatal round struck the insurgent's hand grenades, causing them to explode.

The repulse of the guerrillas at Kirchschlag indicated the need for more Austrian troops to protect the border. The government responded with additional infantry, cavalry, and artillery. Troops were even drawn from Austria's westernmost provinces. Meanwhile, insurgent operations against the Austrian paramilitary forces continued unabated. The guerrillas launched attacks against posts in the villages of Agendorf and Mattersdorf, a short distance from Ödenburg, and against the post in the hamlet of Bernstein, near Kirchschlag.

As the insurgent activity surged, Austria's army could do little but send more troops to the border. The towns of Alhau, Neudau, Wörth, and Burgnau all came under attack. On September 23, guerrillas destroyed a section of the railroad line from Hungary to Vienna at Bruck, severing the major transportation link between Austria and Hungary. The sabotage was followed that night by an assault by armed Hungarian railroad workers and insurgents. The workers attacked the company of Austrian soldiers charged with protecting the rail link from the rear, while a hundred guerrillas made a frontal assault on the unit's position. Entrenched on the east bank of the Leitha River, the Austrians executed a skillful withdrawal to the nearby Leitha Canal, southeast of Bruck. After reassembling, the company launched a vicious counterattack against the Hungarians, a difficult operation made more so because it was conducted in darkness. But during a three-hour pitched battle, the troops drove the guerrillas not only out of the Austrians' former positions but also out of the houses in the immediate vicinity.

During the September clashes, the Allied Military Control Commission denied the Austrian army permission to enter Burgenland; it was still searching for a peaceful solution to a situation that was at a violent impasse. October brought little respite in fighting but important political decisions. The Allied commission nominally took over administration of Burgenland. Then on October 13, in Venice, mediation efforts underwritten by the Italian government resulted in an agreement between Hungary and Austria known as the Venice Protocol. The agreement provided for a Burgenland plebiscite to be held in December and called for the cessation of insurgent activity.

The guerrillas, however, realizing how the planned plebiscite would limit their ability to influence the Burgenland population, refused to abide by the agreement. On October 20, the insurgents renewed their attacks. They were dealing from a position of increased strength because Austrian gendarmes had evacuated their posts in the province, and been replaced by Hungarian paramilitary forces.

Equally ominous were the actions of the Hungarian government, which had brought the insurgents under more overt control. The Hungarian army also began to exercise more formal authority over the guerrillas. The new "gendarmes" received their supplies from army logistic units, and Hungarian guerrilla units received field communications equipment and the use of military telephone networks for better command and control. Some insurgent bands were even equipped with armored vehicles. By the end of October the entire Hungarian insurgent effort had been reorganized and was operating along formal military lines.

Combat further intensified in early November. On the first, fighting broke out at the Schoeffer Bridge, southeast of the village of Haideggendorf. It cost the Austrians nine dead and eighteen wounded, among them several civilians. The same day, near the town of Katzelsdorf, a skirmish occurred in which the Hungarians reputedly suffered considerable casualties. Then on the fourth, Austrian troops repulsed an insurgent attack on the railroad bridge near Neudorfel. This was too much. The Allied Military Control Commission had finally had enough. On the third anniversary of the armistice that ended World War I, the eleventh of November, the commission invited the Austrian army into Burgenland.

It was a moment for which Austrian officers and soldiers had been waiting. They now had virtually unrestricted authority to impose a military solution on a situation that political negotiations had failed to resolve.

At 8 A.M. on November 13, four columns of Austrian troops entered northern Burgenland. Half of the army's brigades participated in the advance, with each column composed of infantry, gendarmes (to take over police duties), cavalry, engineers, technical units, and artillery. The Austrian advance was cautious, and the artillery sections moved forward in stages, so as to provide con-

By the end of October the entire Hungarian insurgent effort was operating along formal military lines.

tinuous fire support, if needed.

The brigades were scheduled to reach their final objectives by the evening of November 14, but the advance was slower than anticipated. Nevertheless, the troops proceeded in good order. An Austrian newspaper correspondent marching with one of the columns noted the techniques the army employed and wrote favorably of the unit's professionalism. Other newspapers reported that the troops were conducting themselves in an exemplary manner.

As the soldiers wended their way along village and town streets during the march, Burgenlanders enthusiastically welcomed them. The Austrian civilian administration almost immediately began to take over authority from the military command. The government reopened railroad lines behind the advancing units, and telephone and telegraph service, interrupted by insurgents, was fully restored.

On November 16, a U.S. Army military attaché reported that the troops' advance was progressing smoothly without any kind of disturbance. He considered the behavior of the soldiers to be excellent and also wrote: "The attitude towards Austria around Ödenburg is becoming more and more favorable. The cause of this change is the lack of friction in the occupation of Burgenland by the Austrian troops and growing disgust with Hungarian tactics."

Success in southern Burgenland, however, was not assured because, as the Austrians secured northern territory, insurgents continued their activities in various southern locales. On November 23, for example, guerrillas there made unauthorized corn and cattle requisitions from local farmers. Again, on the twenty-fifth, the opening day of the sec-

ond phase of Austrian operations, reports circulated of guerrillas intimidating editors and booksellers who would not print or distribute insurgent propaganda.

In spite of such activity, the second phase of operations went ahead unimpeded. A review of the events of the first phase revealed no need for any plan revisions. Again four columns using elements from three brigades marched south. Anticipated resistance did not develop, and the advance into southern Burgenland was relatively uneventful. Hungarian guerrillas did not contest the brigades as they moved from town to town. Terrain in the south, however, was less conducive to rapid movement than in the north. The weather also began to become uncooperative, and at the end of the month snow began to fall. Nevertheless, the southern Burgenlanders were just as enthusiastic to see the Austrians as were the northerners. The press again reported that the inhabitants were glad to be liberated from the terror of the Hungarian guerrilla bands.

On the last day of November, the army completed occupation of Burgenland. But this did not mean that the insurgency was over: Just because the insurgents did not oppose the march of the Austrian army did not mean that they had given up. In fact, the hard part of the army's task was just beginning.

Roving bands of guerrillas continued to pose a threat throughout the province, although the army's mere presence deterred them from being a cause of major trouble. Instead the army's test came during the period between combat and true peace. The exuberance of marching into a town to the cheers of joyful inhabitants would not last during the cold, wet days of boring guard duty.

Unguarded moments could be disastrous if the insurgents chose to contest the Austrian occupation—even if the guerrillas overwhelmed only a small group of soldiers. The morale of soldiers was at stake, as was the confidence in the army of Burgenlanders and Austrians. Although leftists in Austria were firmly behind the soldiers, those on the right still doubted the army's effectiveness. Some Austrians were still not convinced that an army was even needed; perhaps a strong gendarmerie was all that was required to ensure the security of the small landlocked country. The army's performance up to this point, however, augured well for its future.

The conduct of the soldiers was no less important off duty than on. Anyone in uniform was subjected to close scrutiny by Burgenlanders, who did not know just what to expect from their new protectors. They still had the opportunity to voice their opinion in the plebiscite, and every soldier therefore became the object of their special interest. A drunk man in uniform reeling down a street, or one suspected of stealing, could swing one vote or more to Hungary.

On November 30, the military government that the Austrians had established in northern Burgenland was terminated, and administration was turned over to civilians, although troops remained throughout the area. Then on December 5, the Allied Military Control Commission pronounced Burgenland free of guerrillas, which turned out to be a prematurely optimistic judgment, and the mettle of the soldiers continued to be tested.

Rumors were rife. On December 8, 1921, for example, word spread that regular Hungarian troops and gendarmes were still active in Ödenburg. Purportedly eight hundred students from schools in the vicinity of insurgents from the Hejjas guerrilla band were reinforcing the Hungarian army and gendarmerie.

Encounters between the Austrian and Hungarian armies also took place. On December 12, a Hungarian unit captured an Austrian patrol. The captors released the Austrians three days later, but two of the prisoners had been so badly beaten during their captivity that they had to be sent to the hospital.

Indeed, the American military attaché in Budapest sounded a disturbing alarm on December 13. He reported that the Hungarians planned to overrun Burgenland with several thousand guerrillas

Burgenland
after December 1921
Plebiscite

BAKER VAIL

and students who were to threaten and terrorize the inhabitants so as to prevent them from going to the polls. It was rumored in the streets that if the plebiscite went against Hungary a "new and terrible guerrilla war" would be launched from Ödenburg. The attaché pointed out that the insurgents, who were concentrated in Ödenburg and Szombathely, were in good positions to strike effectively.

The threats, which heightened the awareness and alertness of the Austrian army, came to naught. The plebiscite held in mid-December was a significant victory for Austria, except in Ödenburg. Although the area around the town voted 54.6 percent to 45.6 percent to join Austria, the town and its immediate suburbs voted by a 2-to-1 margin to go with Hungary. Ödenburg thus became a Hungarian protrusion into the Austrian province of Burgenland. The city subsequently became known as Sopron.

The plebiscite, however, did not stop a new enemy from appearing on the scene—inadequate logistical support for the Austrian garrisons in Burgenland. This was a fight for the soldiers' morale and welfare. It also became a test for the leadership in a unionized army where military "shop stewards" wielded influence, especially in the realm of soldiers' rights and well-being.

Rail cars, motor vehicles, and, on short hauls, horse-drawn wagons were used to supply the troops. Army units sustained by rail generally had fewer problems. Most organizations, however, were not so fortunate. They depended on supply trucks, which were in continuous use and quickly wore out. Replacement parts were hard to obtain, and the generally poor condition of streets and roads exacerbated the situation. The dangerous routes required drivers to be extra careful. Ironically, the greatest loss of soldiers during the entire campaign came when two truck accidents claimed the lives of seventeen servicemen.

The Austrian army's supply and administrative system was clearly not up to meeting the soldiers' needs, which lowered troop morale and led to deteriorating unit performance. Food and clothing, especially important during the winter of 1921-22, were supplied on an irregular basis. Essentials such as soap became scarce. Mail—an important morale booster—was slow to be delivered. Pay problems also worsened, as troops complained that Burgenland postmasters were not accustomed to sending funds by mail. In many instances soldiers were forced to wait to deliver their pay to their families by hand.

Finally, on March 1, 1922, needed relief arrived. The Austrian government replaced 75 percent of its troops in Burgenland with fresh formations. Fifty percent of these replacement troops returned to their home garrisons in July. The remaining army units in the province redeployed to their permanent stations, as Burgenlander recruits joined locally formed and stationed units.

Thus ended the Austrian army's eleven-month Burgenland campaign. Its successful conclusion and the acquisition of the province provided Austria with a permanent boundary with Hungary that still exists. Territorially the city-province of Vienna gained a buffer zone between itself and Hungary. And economically Austria gained the province's wine-producing region and the tourist attraction of the large Neusiedler See.

From a military standpoint, the Burgenland campaign gave the Austrian army a unique opportunity to prove itself. Despite restrictions placed upon it by the peace treaty of St. Germain-en-Laye, time and again in Burgenland and along its border the soldiers of the leftist Austrian republic, such as Franz Samotny, had proved themselves competent soldiers. Possibly more important, the country's citizens, regardless of political persuasion, began to appreciate the need for an effective armed force. The question of whether or not Austria required an army was never again raised.

RAYMOND E. BELL JR. is a retired U.S. Army brigadier general. He writes from Cornwall-on-Hudson, New York.

Before his days as head of the **Luftwaffe**, Hermann Göring, a World War I fighter ace, wrote a revealing essay on tactics used by the German air force in the Great War.

TACTICAL EXERCISES

Jagdgeschwader Tactics

Translated and edited by O'Brien Browne

Although Hermann Göring is now famous—or infamous—as the leader of Adolf Hitler's Luftwaffe *and at one time as the second in command of the Third Reich in World War II, in the previous war he was a twenty-two-victory ace who earned the coveted* Orden Pour le Mérite. *An intelligent officer and a fine organizer, he commanded the prestigious* Jagdgeschwader *(Fighter Wing) I, which had been led by "Red Baron" Manfred von Richthofen until his death in combat on April 21, 1918. Göring's time as a wing commander provided him with the opportunity to develop air combat strategy and tactics.*

After World War I, Göring wrote a fascinating and revealing treatise describing Jagdgeschwader *tactics that had been used with great success by the German air force during the Great War. His article appeared in the 1923 anthology* In der Luft unbesiegt: Erlebsisse im Weltkrieg (Unconquered in the Air: Experiences in the World War), *published only in German. This is the first time it has appeared in English.*

At the time of writing, the Treaty of Versailles forbade the creation of a German air service. Göring bemoans this in the text and wistfully dreams of a day when a new generation of German leaders will recapture the lost glory of their nation's airmen. Ominously, Göring foresees a coming showdown with the Allies. This gives the text a special sinister foreboding, even while it remains historically significant regarding the development of aerial combat tactics.

In the World War, "battle" or combat flying came about after we had rapidly come to the realization that the fight against a powerfully destructive enemy air force could not be carried out from the ground, but rather that we had to fight them airplane against airplane. Everybody set about building, with increasing rapidity, small aircraft (single-seat fighters), which offered—with great maneuverability and speed along with good weaponry (machine guns)—the possibility of destroying the opponent in aerial combat. Now, after this tool had been developed, it was possible to use it in a tactically correct manner. Nobody, however, had any experience with this. And thus there were at first only a few especially distinguished fliers who could be trusted with these combat aircraft, and who, following their own judgment, now flew about the airspace in these craft in order to seek out and destroy the opponent, and in this way carried out the fight themselves by hunting on their own. From this the name "pursuit flying" ["*Jadgfliegerei*"] originated. Because the opponent, however, utilized the same means, and as a consequence of his greater numbers very quickly wrested aerial superiority for himself, we also had to start building up combat aircraft in great numbers. At this point, the experiences of our bold heroes [Lieutenant Max] Immelmann, [Captain Oswald] Bölcke and others offered the tactical basis. This transformed itself into the creation of the combat flight (3 airplanes), the combat wing (6 airplanes), and finally the combat squadron (12 airplanes). In July 1917, the first *Jagdgeschwader* was created on a trial basis, and consisted of 4 fighter squadrons [*Jagdstaffeln*]. Two reasons were decisive here. First, it was apparent that the Englishmen often simultaneously appeared during their aerial battles in Flanders with over 50 airplanes, and we could not oppose this mass with any combat group led in a unified manner at the appropriate strength. Second, there originated in the person of *Rittmeister Freiherr* von Richthofen a fighter pilot whose excellent, wide-ranging leadership skills had to be put to better use than that which was possible at a *Jagdstaffel*. After this, several other *Jagdgeschwader* were later created. The purpose of these *Jagdgeschwader* was to deploy them at the hot points of the major embattled areas of the front in order to break enemy aerial superiority there and to secure command of the air for our own observation aircraft. The tactics of these *Jagdgeschwader* were extremely complicated. Yet it was possible to bring around 50-60 airplanes into battle according to a unified system and clear rules. It remained, however, the exception that the entire squadron was deployed in close formation. Usually, flight formation deployment by the commander was successful. In general, *Jagdgeschwader* tactics also included the following:

Based on continual dispatches, the commander had to be certain which forces he had to deploy in order to command airspace. It mostly happened that one *Staffel* was deployed after the other, and in this way there was always some kind of a force or another patrolling over the front. Obviously, this should not appear as if this were merely concerned with barrage flights [defensive patrolling up and down one's front lines to prevent enemy aircraft from crossing over]. Barrage flights very quickly exhausted and deadened the fighting spirit of the *Staffeln*. For these reasons, deployment was only limited to times of increased enemy aerial activity, and to the advances of our own observation aircraft and our accompanying ground attacks. Only in especially important cases was the *Jagdgeschwader* led in close formation into battle. In general the tactics were that each *Staffel* came together on its own and remained together in close formation. Then these *Staffeln*, in close

Top: Yellow-nose Pfalz D.IIIs of Jagdstaffel 10, one of four squadrons consituting Manfred Freiherr von Richthofen's Jagdgeschwader I, line up at Awoingt Aerodrome in November 1917. Above: First Lieutenant Hermann Göring, third and last "ringmaster" of the Red Baron's Flying Circus, beside his all white Fokker D.VIIF in October 1918.

formation, grouped together around the commander—flying at the lowest level and in the most forward position—in such a way that one *Staffel* would follow him tightly at the center while a second one was above and to the right, the third above and to the left and formed up somewhat toward the rear, while the fourth *Staffel* could be seen above the other three, acting as a main reserve and cover. An attack by such a *Geschwader* had to be carried out with incredible force and fighting vigor. The commander sought out the object to be attacked and then gave the signal to engage. While up to this point the *Geschwader* itself formed a tightly formed mass in flight, it was possible, in order to develop the attack in good time, to increase distance to be more maneu-

verable for a man-to-man fight. Then it usually happened that the middle *Staffel* swooped down into the center of the opposing squadron and attempted to scatter them while simultaneously both of the outer flights attempted to surround and cut off the opponent, while the reserve *Staffel* covered them from further enemy attacks from above or dived on those cut off, or on single machines separated from the general field of battle, in order to destroy them. When the battle was over, the flight leaders came together by flying around a specified area in order to collect the *Staffeln*, which had been scattered during the fight, into a tight formation once again. They then led them to the *Geschwader* commander in the same formation as before, so that the *Geschwader* was united

for a new battle.

Besides these aerial battles, the *Geschwader* had still another task to fulfill. If it were possible for them to gain aerial superiority and to sweep the opponent himself out of the airspace, then it was the commander's commendable duty to involve his *Geschwader* in the battles on the ground. This occurred in such a way that upon his signal the four *Staffeln* formed up in a broad formation and, in a dive, went after ground targets: marching columns, artillery being moved up, battery positions in the rear, and above all the tanks which were so dangerous to our infantry.

In this short outline concerning *Jagdgeschwader* tactics, I want to limit myself to only mentioning what was actually done in the World War, and I do not want to get into how, based upon the experiences which have been made, the tactics of the *Jagdgeschwader* would have been further elaborated. But we all know that, as concerns the activities of the air force, still undreamed of possibilities would have lain before us, and that which was said above merely forms the first application as well as the foundation of the tactics and composition of the *Jagdgeschwader*. Now, because of the disgraceful Treaty of Versailles, we temporarily do not have an air force at our disposal; thus it appears futile to deal with the further tactical problems of this weapon. This shall be the grand task of the leaders who have been summoned to the future gigantic struggle, the showdown over Germany's freedom, to lead our fighting squadrons to the same victories and the same successes, such as Richthofen understood when he made the first German *Jagdgeschwader* a terror to its enemies.

O'BRIEN BROWNE is a freelance writer based in Heidelberg, Germany.

Forty years after North Vietnamese patrol boats reportedly attacked U.S. destroyers, the sequence of events surrounding the Gulf of Tonkin incident is finally coming into clearer focus.

'Received Information

by Edward J. Drea

Editor's note: This article differs from those that MHQ *normally publishes. We expect our historians to answer the questions who, what, where, and when—as well as to provide readers with how and why. For reasons that will become apparent, however, Edward Drea's treatment of the August 4, 1964, Gulf of Tonkin incident is by necessity more of an incomplete chronology than a history. Many of President Lyndon B. Johnson's detractors have long claimed he escalated American participation in the Vietnam War through fraud by insisting that U.S. naval forces had been attacked on the night of August 4 when, in fact, they had not been fired upon. This event has been cited by a number of observers as the beginning of an age when Americans began to distrust the federal government. On the fortieth anniversary of the incident, it is time to update what we know about the event's who, what, and when.*

In the last several years, more information has been revealed through the declassification of some documents involving sensitive U.S. radio intercepts of North Vietnamese communications. We asked Ed Drea to write an article that would give our readers the flavor of the confusion during some of the most tense hours in U.S. history, when a shooting situation that occurred in one time zone sparked rapid-fire questions, analyses, and decisions in three other time zones. Drea is a contract historian at the Pentagon, hence the need to publish what MHQ *has never before printed, the stock Department of Defense disclaimer: "The views expressed in this article are those of the author and do not reflect the official policy or position of the Department of Defense or the U.S. Government."*

U.S. NAVAL HISTORICAL CENTER

Darkness was falling over the Gulf of Tonkin on August 4, 1964, when at 8:40 P.M. Saigon time (8:40 A.M. Eastern Daylight Time [EDT]) the destroyer USS *Maddox*, on patrol, issued a high-priority message, or critic report: "Received information indicating attack by PGM/P-4 [North Vietnamese navy PT-boats, or Swatows]. Proceeding Southeast at best speed."

The source of the information was a U.S. field-site warning dispatched exactly one hour earlier, at 7:40 Saigon time, by flash precedence to *Maddox*, its fellow destroyer *Turner Joy*, and other addressees. Partially declassified in March 2003, the message reads: "Haiphong informed Vessel T142 (Swatow Class) to make ready for military operations the night of 04 August. The sister ship, T-146 has also received similar orders. Message exchanges indicate that all efforts are being made to include MTB (Motor Torpedo Boat) T333 in this operation, as

Indicating Attack'

A North Vietnamese patrol boat streaks across the Gulf of Tonkin during the August 2, 1964, attack on USS Maddox. Two days later, a reported attack against Maddox and another U.S. destroyer, Turner Joy, led to tense decision-making in Washington.

Commander Herbert L. Ogier, had cause for alarm. Swatows were Chinese-manufactured motor gunboats capable of making twenty-eight knots. The eighty-three-foot-long vessels carried a crew of thirty men armed with 37mm and 14.5mm guns, as well as surface search radar and depth charges. P 4s were Soviet-built motor torpedo boats that could exceed fifty knots. Though smaller and with an eleven-man crew, the P-4 carried two torpedoes with a range of forty-five hundred yards. The warning was all the more ominous because one of the North Vietnamese navy vessels identified in the message—*T-333*, assigned to Division 3 of PT Squadron 135—had attacked *Maddox* thirty miles off the North Vietnamese coast two days earlier.

Just after 4 P.M. on August 2, the three P-4 PT-boats had closed on *Maddox* at speeds approaching fifty knots. The first boat launched a torpedo, then broke off as the two other vessels bore in on their target. One PT-boat fired two torpedoes at *Maddox*, but was hit by the destroyer's return fire. Meanwhile the first boat reengaged the destroyer, maneuvering to within two thousand yards while launching a torpedo and firing its 14.5mm guns at the U.S. ship. *Maddox*'s guns heavily damaged the boat and killed its commanding officer. Around 4:30 P.M. the North Vietnamese turned toward shore. Shortly afterward, U.S. Navy planes from the aircraft carrier *Ticonderoga* attacked the withdrawing boats, leaving one dead in the water. During the fighting, *T-333* suffered damage to an auxiliary engine that left it with a low lubrication oil pressure reading but otherwise fit for action. Only a single round of North Vietnamese fire hit the destroyer. Anti-aircraft fire from the P-4s, however, hit one U.S. Navy plane, forcing it to divert to Da Nang. There could be no doubt about an attack launched in broad daylight that had inflicted damage on both sides.

What happened in the Gulf of Tonkin on August 4, however,

soon as additional oil can be obtained for that vessel."

Just three minutes later the same unit transmitted another warning to *Maddox*: "At 0910Z [Zulu, or Greenwich Mean, time], Haiphong informed Vessel T142 of DeSoto destroyers location: Time 1345 (Golf [Hanoi time]) 106-19-30E/19-36-23N." Haiphong's tracking was accurate.

Aboard *Maddox*, Captain John J. Herrick, commander of the two-destroyer task group CTG 72.1, and the destroyer's skipper, remains shrouded in controversy. Did North Vietnamese patrol boats attack *Maddox* and *Turner Joy*? Did a naval battle occur that night, or was it rather the case, as President Lyndon B. Johnson told Under Secretary of State George Ball a few days later, that "those dumb, stupid sailors were just shooting at flying fish"? The issue is more than one of historical curiosity, because on the basis of the second attack Johnson ordered retaliatory airstrikes against North Vietnamese targets and secured from Congress the Gulf of Tonkin Resolution, which he thereafter used to validate his decisions to escalate the American role in the war in Southeast Asia.

North Vietnamese authorities, including no less a figure than General Vo Nguyen Giap, vice premier for defense in 1964, have consistently denied an attack took place on August 4; an official North Vietnamese military history of the conflict labels the engagement a U.S. fabrication. Perhaps of greater importance, at the time of the incident several U.S. senators disputed the administration's account, and hearings before the Senate Committee on Foreign Relations in February 1968 aired serious doubts that a second attack had actually occurred. In 1972 Dr. Louis Tordella, then deputy director of the National Security Agency, concluded that certain of the intercepted North Vietnamese messages referred to events of August 2, not August 4, a view endorsed in 1984 by Ray S. Cline, the CIA's deputy director for intelligence at the time of the action. Even former secretary of defense Robert S. McNamara, the chief architect of U.S. military escalation in Vietnam during 1965, appears to have changed his mind. As late as 1995 he believed that the attack seemed "probable but not certain," but in 1999 McNamara wrote that there was no second attack.

First-person accounts of what happened differ as well. Carrier pilots defending *Maddox* the night of August 4 strafed the waters where the enemy boats were reported, but most, including Medal of Honor recipient Commander James Stockdale, did not see any hostile craft. According to the debriefing report sent to Washington, another pilot, the commanding officer of the attack squadron, flying between seven hundred and fifteen hundred feet over the destroyers, spotted gun flashes and light antiaircraft bursts at his altitude as well as a "snakey" high-speed wake 1½ miles ahead of *Maddox*. The command pilot himself only recalled a short debriefing in which he had answered "no" when asked if he had observed enemy PT-boats. On the other hand, several crew members aboard the destroyers saw torpedo wakes, ships' running lights, searchlights, and gunfire flashes.

Amid these allegations and counterclaims, exactly what happened on the night of August 4, 1964, in the Gulf of Tonkin will likely remain unresolved until the United States and Vietnam completely open their archival material on the incident. There is little chance of that happening in the immediate future, but

Jargon and Messages

Bogey: A visual or radar air contact that is assumed to be enemy

CTF: Carrier Task Force

Critic Report: Crucial intelligence, such as a strong indication of the outbreak of war

Flash Precedence: A category of messages reserved for initial enemy contacts or matters of extreme urgency

NMCC: National Military Command Center (the Pentagon)

PACOM: Pacific Command (Hawaii)

Skunk: A visual or radar contact on the surface of the water that is assumed to be enemy

The Tank: Pentagon conference room where the Joint Chiefs of Staff confer or receive briefings

based on the incomplete but recently expanded record, a chronological review of participants' actions—from the deck of *Maddox* to the Cabinet Room of the White House—will at least provide a better picture of what U.S. civilian and military leaders thought was happening.

Shortly after assuming the presidency in November 1963, Johnson instructed his senior policymakers to devise covert missions targeting North Vietnam in order to discourage the regime's support of Viet Cong operations against the U.S.–backed Saigon government. Their answer was OPLAN (Operations Plan) 34-A, a series of commando raids beginning in January 1964 against selected targets in North Vietnam, including raids on coastal areas by high-speed patrol boats. Following an early March 1964 trip to South Vietnam, Secretary of Defense McNamara recommended stepped-up retaliatory measures against North Vietnam, which were adopted on March 17 as National Security Action Memorandum No. 288.

As U.S.–directed covert operations conducted by South Vietnamese boat crews and raiders intensified in the late spring and early summer of 1964, North Vietnam's Politburo of the Party Central Committee instructed the country's armed forces in June to destroy any enemy violating their territory. On July 6, the North Vietnamese navy went on wartime status, and to counter the OPLAN 34-A raids along the coast, naval headquarters established a forward headquarters under Nguyen Ba Phat, deputy commander of the navy, near Quang Khe, a PT base located between Vinh and Dong Hoi, the area hardest hit by South Vietnamese commandos. Naval units were placed on high alert, sailors and cadre were recalled from leave, and torpedo boats conducted familiarization and operational training. The general staff and navy headquarters ordered the 135th Torpedo Boat Squadron, stationed at Ben Thuy and Quang Khe, to attack any enemy vessel invading territorial waters.

Concerned that the North Vietnamese buildup would make future commando raids ashore prohibitively expensive, on July 24 McNamara asked his military advisers if offshore bombardment might serve the same purpose. In the early morning hours of July 31, four OPLAN 34-A vessels shelled Hon Me and Hon Nieu, islands north of Vinh. The two boats bombarding Hon Me were in turn attacked by North Vietnamese gunboats and pursued unsuccessfully by Swatow *T-142*.

Simultaneously, the U.S. Navy was running electronic intelligence collection sweeps, code-named "Desoto," along North Vietnam's coast. On July 15, Admiral U.S. Grant Sharp, commander in chief, Pacific (CINCPAC), requested a Desoto patrol. Washington approved it, and two days later *Maddox* received its mission orders. The destroyer entered the Gulf of Tonkin on July 31 and proceeded to its designated patrol track parallel to the North Vietnamese coastline. As McNamara has pointed out, the Desoto patrols sailed only in international waters conducting electronic reconnaissance and were substantially different from the OPLAN 34-A combat operations that routinely violated North Vietnamese territorial waters. While the missions of the two were unlike in nature, both involved "enemy" warships transiting the Gulf of Tonkin and approaching the North Vietnamese coast. Hanoi could understandably regard a U.S. destroyer's presence, in some cases only eight nautical miles offshore, as a backup should the smaller OPLAN 34-A vessels find themselves in trouble. Thus, early on August 2, North Vietnamese naval headquarters reinforced Hon Me with three P-4s and ordered preparations for battle. That afternoon the P-4s attacked *Maddox*.

North Vietnamese authorities have since claimed that their local naval commanders acted on their own initiative during the Gulf of Tonkin incidents. But the presence of the deputy commander of the navy on scene, as well as intercepted messages that indicate a higher headquarters in Haiphong was routinely passing orders and maintaining a communications link with the forward PT-boat bases, suggests that control was more highly centralized than believed then or now. On August 2, 1964, for example, Lyndon Johnson also concluded that "an overeager North Vietnamese boat commander" or a local shore station, rather than a senior commander, might have miscalculated in ordering the attack and so decided against any retaliation. As LBJ reported to the American people

Zulu Time

The U.S. military uses a single time zone to identify its worldwide message traffic. According to the system, Greenwich Mean Time (GMT) is denoted by the letter Z, phonetically pronounced "Zulu." The time is converted to GMT and appears on a message written with the month, day, and military-style, or twenty-four-hour, time. For example, 7:40 P.M. Saigon time on August 4 would be written as Aug041140Z. The same Zulu time would be written for August 4, 7:40 A.M. Eastern Daylight Time (Saigon time and EDT differ by twelve hours).

Above left: At the time of the August 2 attack, USS Maddox *was on an intelligence-gathering mission thirty miles off North Vietnam's coast. Left:* Maddox's *executive officer, Lt. Cmdr. Dempster M. Jackson, kneels next to the only damage the destroyer sustained in that attack: a machine gun bullet hole. Far left: Captain John J. Herrick (left), standing next to* Maddox *captain Commander Herbert Ogier, was in charge of a two-destroyer task group during the alleged August 4 attack.*

the following day, however, he did double the strength of the Desoto patrol, provide it with air cover, and order the commanders of the two destroyers and combat aircraft not only to defend against patrol boat attacks but also to "counter attack and destroy any force attempting to repeat the attacks."

On the night of August 3, two OPLAN 34-A PT-boats fired more than seven hundred rounds of 57mm and 40mm ammunition at a North Vietnamese radar site near Vinh Son while another boat shelled a security post at the mouth of the Ron River. North Vietnamese ashore returned fire on the single boat, and a North Vietnamese navy patrol boat pursued it in vain. The same night, the commander of the Seventh Fleet, Vice Adm. Roy L. Johnson, recommended to Admiral Thomas H. Moorer, commander in chief, Pacific Fleet, that the Desoto patrols be ended after the August 4 mission. Moorer disagreed, contending that terminating the patrol two days after the attack would indicate a lack of American resolve. The president, after all, had publicly announced that the ongoing patrol would continue, and the Joint Chiefs of Staff (JCS) had already cabled Admiral Sharp to continue the patrol, reinforced by *Turner Joy*, and avoid approaches to the North Vietnamese coast while OPLAN 34-A operations were underway.

On the morning of August 4, while preparing for the day's mission, Herrick informed Admiral Johnson that various intelligence sources suggested the North Vietnamese directly linked the OPLAN raids and the Desoto patrols and would consequently treat the United States as an enemy. Nevertheless, higher headquarters and the White House seemed to accept the risk of another attack, and the patrol continued. Given these circumstances, Herrick took the field unit's warning of impending North Vietnamese action very seriously.

The field site's 7:40 P.M. Saigon time warning to *Maddox* of indications of an imminent attack reached the Defense Intelligence Agency Indications Center in the Pentagon by phone at 8:13 A.M. on August 4. While the watch officer was on the phone, the message itself arrived from a field unit stating there were "imminent plans of DRV [Democratic Republic of Vietnam] naval action possibly against DeSoto mission." Around 9 A.M., the Indications Center team chief briefed General Earle G. Wheeler, chairman of the JCS, and Secretary McNamara. Wheeler was to attend a meeting in New York City with the *New*

York Times editorial board that morning, and he and McNamara agreed that he should keep the appointment because a sudden cancellation might result in speculation that a military crisis was brewing.

Twelve minutes later, McNamara phoned President Johnson to tell him that *Maddox* was again on alert, reporting the presence of hostile ships and based on "U.S. intercepts of North Vietnamese communications…suspected that an attack seemed imminent." Meanwhile, at 8:36 P.M. Saigon time USS *Ticonderoga* had reported that *Maddox*, then sixty-five miles from the nearest land, had radar fixes

After learning of potential August 4 North Vietnamese attacks, Secretary of Defense Robert McNamara (right) told Secretary of State Dean Rusk (left) that he was "inclined to do much more" than "go after the boats," and that President Lyndon B. Johnson (center) agreed with the tougher position.

on two unidentified surface vessels (skunks) and three unidentified aircraft (bogies). (This report took almost two hours to reach the National Military Command Center, arriving at 10:30 A.M. EDT.) In the dark, moonless night in the Gulf of Tonkin, low clouds and thunderstorms further restricted visibility, leaving *Maddox* dependent on its radar and sonar arrays for data throughout most of the action that followed.

After receiving the destroyer's message about radar contacts, *Ticonderoga* had launched fighter aircraft to protect *Maddox* from possible attack. Thirty-two minutes later, at 10:08 Saigon time, a message relayed from *Maddox* reported that the bogies had dropped off the radar screen and the surface contacts were maintaining a twenty-seven-mile distance without attempting to close on the ship. At 10:34 Rear Adm. Robert B. Moore, commander of Carrier Task Force 77, aboard *Ticonderoga*, signaled: "The two original Skunks opened to 40 miles. Three new Skunks contacted at 13 miles. Closed to 11 miles. Evaluated as hostile. CAP (Combat Air Patrol)/STRIKE/PHOTO [attack aircraft/reconnaissance aircraft] overhead under control of Maddox." Six minutes later *Maddox* flashed, "Commenced fire on closing PT boats."

While these events were transpiring in the Gulf, McNamara, Deputy Secretary of Defense Cyrus R. Vance, Lt. Gen. David A. Burchinal (director of the Joint Staff, JCS), and other military officers had been meeting at the Pentagon since 9:25 A.M. to discuss possible options should the North Vietnamese again attack a U.S. Navy ship in international waters. At 9:43 the president returned from his breakfast meeting with congressional leaders and phoned the secretary of defense for more details of events in the Gulf of Tonkin. McNamara informed him that Admiral Sharp had recommended that the task force commander move closer to shore and be authorized to pursue and destroy any attackers, including airstrikes against naval bases. McNamara thought that a bad idea because it forfeited Washington's ability to control a measured response to North Vietnamese aggression.

President Johnson worried that allowing North Vietnam to shoot first made the United States appear reactive, and he thought "we not only ought to shoot at them, but almost simultaneously pull one of these things that you've been doing—on one of their bridges, or something." McNamara quickly agreed, but still rejected Sharp's wholesale approach. Johnson concurred, but added that he wished there were targets already picked out so planes could "just hit three of them damn quick and go right after them." "We will have that," McNamara assured the president. In fact he had just told Special Presidential Assistant McGeorge Bundy that they should have "a retaliation move against North Vietnam" ready for the president "in the event this attack takes place within the next six to nine hours." Johnson and McNamara decided to discuss those options at a scheduled White House lunch that afternoon.

McNamara then huddled with JCS representatives and Vance at the Pentagon to examine incoming reports of the rapidly developing situation and discuss possible alternative methods of retaliation, such as air attacks against naval bases, airfields, bridges, and POL (petroleum, oil, and lubricant) installations, or the mining of one or more important North Vietnamese ports.

During the meeting, McNamara was repeatedly called away to the phone. At 9:55 he told Secretary of State Dean Rusk that he was "inclined to do much more" than "go after the boats" as Rusk had suggested, and that the president agreed with the tougher position. At 10:19 McNamara phoned Admiral Sharp in Honolulu (where it was 4:19 A.M.) about a possible attack on *Maddox* and was emphatic that the navy could use whatever force it needed to destroy the attacking craft. When Sharp said four aircraft were launched "until an attack happens," McNamara interrupted, "Oh, yes, surely, I understand that, but after the attack happens, you wouldn't feel limited to 8 or 10 or anything like that."

At 10:33 McNamara signed JCS message 7700 to Sharp, which changed the rules of engagement by authorizing U.S. aircraft, previously restricted to operations during daylight hours seaward of the destroyers, to pursue any attackers to within three nautical miles of the North Vietnamese coastline. The same message confirmed earlier verbal orders to the carrier *Constellation* to join *Ticonderoga* in the Gulf.

Twenty minutes later, McNamara again phoned the president to update him based on *Ticonderoga*'s 041236Z (8:36 P.M. Saigon time) message about *Maddox* detecting unidentified planes and ships on its radar and the carrier launching fighter aircraft to protect the destroyer from possible attack. He reassured Johnson that there were ample forces available in the

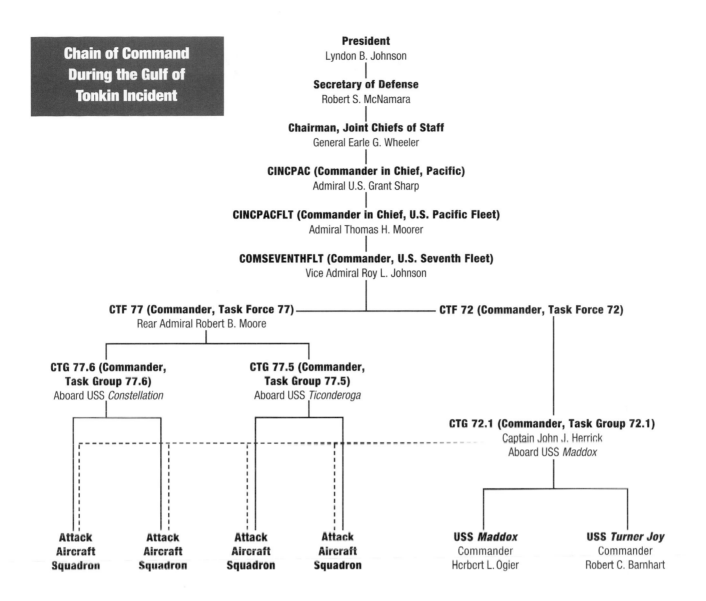

Chain of Command During the Gulf of Tonkin Incident

President
Lyndon B. Johnson

Secretary of Defense
Robert S. McNamara

Chairman, Joint Chiefs of Staff
General Earle G. Wheeler

CINCPAC (Commander in Chief, Pacific)
Admiral U.S. Grant Sharp

CINCPACFLT (Commander in Chief, U.S. Pacific Fleet)
Admiral Thomas H. Moorer

COMSEVENTHFLT (Commander, U.S. Seventh Fleet)
Vice Admiral Roy L. Johnson

CTF 77 (Commander, Task Force 77)
Rear Admiral Robert B. Moore

CTF 72 (Commander, Task Force 72)

CTG 77.6 (Commander, Task Group 77.6)
Aboard USS *Constellation*

CTG 77.5 (Commander, Task Group 77.5)
Aboard USS *Ticonderoga*

CTG 72.1 (Commander, Task Group 72.1)
Captain John J. Herrick
Aboard USS *Maddox*

Attack Aircraft Squadron

Attack Aircraft Squadron

Attack Aircraft Squadron

Attack Aircraft Squadron

USS *Maddox*
Commander
Herbert L. Ogier

USS *Turner Joy*
Commander
Robert C. Barnhart

Gulf to retaliate, and explained that for good measure only two hours earlier he had ordered *Constellation* to move down toward South Vietnam. McNamara also promised to give the president a list of targets when he arrived at the White House for their noon meeting. By this time the Pentagon conferees had narrowed potential targets to four options: airstrikes against PT-boats and their bases, against POL targets, against bridges, and against prestige targets, such as steel mills. General Burchinal also informed McNamara that retaliatory attacks could be made at first light in North Vietnam, or around 7 P.M. Washington time.

Meanwhile Burchinal had also been on the phone with CINC-PAC headquarters, alerting Sharp to the changed rules of engagement and evaluating possible reprisal targets. Toward the end of their 10:59 conversation, Sharp said he "just got a report saying that DESOTO Patrol is under continuous torpedo attack." Burchinal had not yet received that message, but promptly told McNamara, who notified the president two minutes later. The defense secretary asked the president's permission to get Rusk and Bundy to the Pentagon to "go over these retaliatory actions." With little other information available on the fighting in the Gulf, Johnson agreed. McNamara then phoned Rusk, informed him of developments, and asked him to come to the Pentagon.

McGeorge Bundy joined Rusk at the 11:40 meeting in the Secretary's Dining Room in the Pentagon. McNamara briefed them on target options, discussed retaliatory measures, and with Bundy thrashed out the pros and cons of limited airstrikes and mining the North Vietnamese coast. McNamara also told General Curtis LeMay, sitting in for the absent Wheeler, that the JCS should prepare recommendations for immediate action as well as proposals for the next 2½ days. Burchinal had again contacted Sharp at 11:18 and told him in circumlocutory language over an open phone line that contemplated actions involved something "more severe than going right in and picking up secondaries." The two officers agreed strikes at first light were preferable.

At 12:04 the meeting broke up. McNamara continued discussions with Vance, Bundy, and Rusk in his office while the JCS resumed deliberations in the Secretary's Dining Room. The chiefs had narrowed alternatives to three: sharp air attacks against a variety of targets, continuing pressure by mining the coast, or a combination of both. At 12:20 McNamara, Rusk, and Bundy departed for the White House while Vance went to ask the chiefs whether it would make any difference if retaliatory strikes were conducted at first light. After learning from them that it would make no difference, Vance left for the White House at 12:25. The JCS continued meeting until 1:49 and directed Burchinal to call McNamara at the White House to recommend their option first.

At 12:22 Sharp had updated Burchinal by phone that the North Vietnamese had fired at least nine torpedoes and lost two boats in the attack and that *Constellation* had launched several aircraft, which were at the scene of the action. During their conversation, Sharp was handed another message confirming two enemy craft sunk, ten torpedoes fired, U.S. aircraft overhead, and no U.S. casualties. Based on the number of torpedoes, Sharp suspected that more than three boats were involved in the attack.

Eighteen minutes later, McNamara's group arrived at the White House from the Pentagon and interrupted a National Security Council (NSC) meeting about the situation in Cyprus, where fighting had broken out between Greeks and Turks. McNamara briefed participants on what was known about developments in the Gulf of Tonkin, and Rusk informed them that he, McNamara, and the JCS were preparing alternatives for response, but these were not yet ready. Following the NSC meeting, at 1:04 Rusk, McNamara, Bundy, Vance, and Central Intelligence Agency Director John McCone joined President Johnson for lunch.

After another twenty minutes, McNamara phoned General Burchinal for an update on the unfolding situation. The general reported the chiefs' unanimous recommendation that three PT bases south of the 20th parallel and POL facilities at Vinh and Phuc Loi be attacked. He then added that another intercept claimed an "enemy boat wounded and an enemy plane falling from the sky." The decryption, recently declassified,

read: "At 041154Z Swatow Class PGM T-142 reported to My Duc (19-52-45N 105-57E) that an enemy aircraft was observed falling into the sea. Enemy vessel perhaps wounded."

Alarmed about the reported shootdown, McNamara told Burchinal to contact Sharp for an up-to-the-minute account of the engagement and call him back. He then informed the president of the latest intelligence.

During the general and admiral's conversation, Sharp could add nothing for Burchinal except "some indication" that a U.S. aircraft might have been hit by enemy fire. He was aware of the intercept and promised to call back with further details. About half an hour later, Sharp phoned Burchinal only to say that he was unable to contact the task force by voice. The steady stream of flash precedence messages up and down the chain of command by this time had overloaded the military communications circuit, forcing Sharp to prohibit CINCPAC from sending further messages at flash precedence. Even so, communications throughout the day were consistently slower than McNamara and Sharp expected, with repeated delays caused by clarifying events, transmitting orders, and making decisions.

To further complicate the situation, Sharp also told Burchinal that the latest report from Herrick, commander of the destroyer task force, questioned the reported contacts and number of torpedoes fired because *Maddox* had no visual sightings of North Vietnamese patrol boats. The message, sent from *Maddox* at 1:27 P.M. EDT read: "Review of action makes many reported contacts and torpedoes fired appear doubtful. Freak weather effects on radar and overeager sonarmen may have accounted for many reports. No actual visual sightings by MADDOX. Suggest complete evaluation before any further action taken." Burchinal said he would pass on Herrick's doubts to McNamara.

At 2:08 P.M. EDT, Sharp again called Burchinal to relay Rear Adm. Moore's latest situation report. Moore, then aboard

Critical U.S. Military Communications

Three important August 4, 1964, communications on the Gulf of Tonkin situation motivated the Johnson administration to begin planning retaliatory action against North Vietnam:

Nature of Message	Originator	Time Transmitted	Received in Pentagon (EDT)	President Notified (EDT)
Indication of imminent attack on U.S. destroyers	Field unit	Aug041140Z 7:40 P.M. SAIGON TIME	8:13 A.M.	9:12 A.M.
USS *Maddox* has radar fixes on 2 skunks and 3 bogies	CTF relays	Aug041236Z 8:36 P.M. SAIGON TIME	10:30 A.M.	10:53 A.M.
U.S. destroyers under continuous torpedo attack	Admiral Sharp (phone call)	11:04 A.M. EDT	11:04 A.M.	11:06 A.M.

Note the more than two-hour delay between the USS *Maddox* report of radar fixes and the time President Johnson was informed. In 1964 the military communications and intelligence system in Southeast Asia and the surrounding waters was primitive in comparison to what it became only two years later. Furthermore, the communications system in Hawaii and the Pentagon was only partially automated. Handling of flash precedence messages required some time-consuming labor, time that added to a growing backlog of both flash messages and messages of importance but of lesser urgency.

Ticonderoga, claimed in a message sent thirty-six minutes earlier that three PT-boats had been sunk. Sharp acknowledged that excited sonarmen had probably overestimated the number of torpedoes fired at *Maddox*. Asked if he was "pretty sure" there was a torpedo attack, Sharp replied, "No doubt about that, I think."

One more significant piece of intelligence reached McNamara at the White House early that afternoon. An intercepted message, again from PGM *T-142*, reported shooting at two enemy planes and damaging at least one. "We sacrificed two comrades but all are brave and recognize our obligation," stated the message. According to Lyndon Johnson's recollections, experts said this meant either two men or two boats in the attack group were lost. Certain from this evidence that the North Vietnamese were again attacking U.S. ships on the high seas, the president agreed on a sharp retaliatory strike against four PT-boat bases and the Vinh oil complex. He ruled out an attack on Haiphong and mining operations.

Asked by Johnson how long it would take to execute the strike, McNamara estimated from the information he had received that an attack could be launched in about four hours, at 7 P.M. EDT, which was first light at 7 A.M. August 5, Saigon time. The president suggested McNamara call the JCS to confirm the time, but the defense secretary indicated his preference to work out the details after his return to the Pentagon. At the close of the meeting, Johnson ordered the full NSC to convene at 6:15 to review his decision and a meeting of congressional leaders at 6:45 so he might inform them of his decision.

Upon his return to the Pentagon at 3, McNamara and Vance immediately joined the JCS, who were meeting in the "Tank." McNamara told them that "the President wants the strikes to take place at 7:00 PM Washington time, if possible," and identified the likely targets. They agreed with the objectives and the schedule. While the JCS drafted the execute message for transmission to CINCPAC, doubts about what had actually happened in the Gulf of Tonkin continued to emerge.

With Herrick's 1:27 message in hand and following Johnson's instructions, McNamara phoned Sharp at 4:08 for clarification. Was there a possibility, he asked, that there had been no attack? Sharp, citing an updated summary of Herrick's later 2:48 EDT situation report, acknowledged there was "a slight possibility" because of freak radar echoes, inexperienced sonarmen, and no visual sightings of torpedo wakes.

Herrick's 2:48 message read:

Certain that original ambush was bonafide. Details of action following present a confusing picture. Have interviewed witnesses who made positive visual sightings of cockpit lights or similar passing near MADDOX. Several reported torpedoes were probably boats themselves which were observed to make several close passes on MADDOX. Own ship screw noises on rudders may have accounted for some. At present cannot even estimate number of boats involved. TURNER JOY reports two torpedoes passed near her.

U.S. Retaliatory Airstrikes
All dates are August 5, unless otherwise noted.
Times are Saigon time;
Eastern Daylight Time is 12 hours earlier.

CHINA

Hanoi ⊛

Port Wallut

Haiphong ⊗ Hon Gay

NORTH VIETNAM

Target Hit: 3:25 P.M.

Target Hit: 3:40 P.M.

Gulf of Tonkin

Loc Chau

415 miles

4:05 P.M. August 2: USS *Maddox* under attack

Hon Me

380 miles

HAINAN

Target Hit: 5:15 P.M.

370 miles

Vinh/Phuc Loi

370 miles

Target Hit: 1:25, 4:45 P.M.

10:39 P.M. August 4: *Maddox* and USS *Turner Joy* reportedly under attack

Quang Khe

290 miles

USS *CONSTELLATION* LAUNCH AREA

Planes first depart: 1:00 P.M.

Target Hit: 1:15 P.M.

DMZ

Hue

LAOS

SOUTH VIETNAM

Da Nang

USS *TICONDEROGA* LAUNCH AREA

Planes first depart: 11:35 A.M.

Scale
0 ——— 100
Statue miles

BAKER VAIL

Sharp was at that moment trying to learn more from CINCPAC Fleet and expected an answer within an hour.

That said, McNamara complicated Washington's timing because, he said, "We don't want to release news of what happened without saying what we are going to do; we don't want to say what we are going to do before we do it." The reports had to be reconciled because "We obviously don't want to do it until we are damn sure what happened." Sharp then suggested holding the execute order until he confirmed the incident. With the strikes scheduled for 7, that gave him two hours, leaving one hour for notification to the carriers. Sharp still thought a 7 o'clock launch was possible, if tight, and told Burchinal at 4:40 P.M. EDT that a recent message indicated the North Vietnamese ambush was bonafide, although exact details were still confusing.

With this information in hand, McNamara, Vance, and the JCS met at 4:47 to determine whether an attack had actually taken place. They decided one had, based on five factors:

1. *Turner Joy* was illuminated when fired on by automatic weapons.

2. One of the destroyers observed cockpit lights.

3. PGM *T-142* fired at two U.S. aircraft.

4. The North Vietnamese navy had announced that two of its boats were "sacrificed."

5. Sharp's determination that an attack had occurred.

Despite Lyndon Johnson's effort to keep the lid on the latest incident, at 5:09 McNamara phoned the president to inform him that The Associated Press and United Press International were carrying reports of the "latest PT-boat attack" on their news tickers. He suggested, and Johnson approved, a noncommittal statement confirming the attacks but providing no further details.

At 5:23 Sharp again phoned Burchinal, asking if he had seen the intercept that described the sacrifice of two ships. The general had, but could not tell if it referred to the earlier action of August 2 or the August 4 incident. Sharp was certain it related to the recently concluded fighting and claimed the intercept "pins it down better than anything so far." Burchinal assured Sharp that McNamara too was "satisfied with the evidence." Six minutes later the JCS transmitted the execute order to CINCPAC directing that by 7 P.M. EDT the carriers launch a one-time maximum effort attack against the five PT bases (the northernmost was later canceled because of weather) and the Vinh oil installation.

During their 5:23 phone conversation, Sharp had informed Burchinal that the airstrikes could not be launched until 8 P.M. Washington time because the carriers operated in a different time zone, one hour behind Saigon. The admiral had also told the carriers to use the extra hour to complete preparations for their attacks.

Throughout the day, Admiral Sharp and General Burchinal had repeatedly assured McNamara that it would be a simple matter to launch an airstrike at first light in the Gulf of Tonkin. When this turned out not to be the case, General Wheeler, who had just returned to Washington, instructed Burchinal to tell McNamara that the carriers could not meet the 7 P.M. launch time as promised because they were operating in the different time zone. Since the president intended to address the nation on the airstrikes at 7, McNamara had a serious problem.

At 6:07 EDT Sharp called Burchinal to confirm that the execute message was agreeable to McNamara, which Burchinal assured him it was. The admiral also acknowledged aircraft would be off target by 9 P.M. EDT. When making his calculations, Sharp apparently discounted the toll *Ticonderoga*'s extensive night operations in support of the two destroyers had taken on flight and deck crews, which now had to ready the carrier for a maximum effort.

Eight minutes later, McNamara, along with the president and his other senior civilian advisers and General Wheeler, attended the 538th meeting of the NSC. McNamara briefed the members on the North Vietnamese attacks and told them the administration had decided on airstrikes against five targets. He outlined a four-point program involving airstrikes, sending reinforcements to the region to demonstrate resolve, a presidential announcement of these actions, and a joint congressional resolution in support of these and, if necessary, further actions. United States Information Agency Director Carl Rowan asked exactly what had happened and whether it was certain that an attack had occurred. McNamara answered that "only highly classified information

During the August 4 crisis, Admiral Grant Sharp (right), commander in chief, Pacific, had the difficult task of serving as an intermediary between Pentagon officials and commanders on the U.S. Navy vessels in the Gulf.

nails down the incident," and more would be known from incoming reports and in the morning. A draft joint resolution on Southeast Asia was revised, and the president would make it public as soon as U.S. planes were over their targets, which McNamara assumed would be 9 P.M.

At 6:45 the president met with congressional leaders, and McNamara again summarized what was planned. After briefings by Rusk and McCone, Johnson and his advisers answered a series of questions. The president then summarized his case for congressional concurrence with his decisions and reminded his audience that "We can tuck our tails and run, but if we do these countries will feel all they have to do to scare us is to shoot at the American flag. The question is how do we retaliate." With expressions of support from all present, the president prepared for his 9 P.M. address to the nation.

As the minutes ticked by without further word from CINCPAC that the planes were airborne, McNamara grew increasingly impatient. At 8:39 he phoned Sharp, told him it was forty minutes past the ordered time for takeoff, and instructed him to radio the carriers and find out what was happening. After all, the president expected to make an address to the American people, and "I am holding him back from making it, but we're forty minutes past the time I told him we would launch." Asked how long it would take the planes to reach their targets after launch, Sharp answered "a little over an hour." Minutes passed, and the 9 o'clock airtime came and went.

At 9:09 McNamara again phoned Sharp, who told him the carriers would launch their planes in fifty minutes. "Oh, my God," gasped McNamara. Sharp then said the planes would be over target at 11 P.M. EDT. The conversation became more and more confused as McNamara tried to pin Sharp down. Was it two hours to the closest target? Sharp assumed that this meant the last TOT (time over target). With a 10 P.M. EDT launch, what was the first TOT? Sharp had no idea. Could the president say at 10, the time of launch, that the air action was in progress against gunboats and their supporting facilities? That, said Sharp, was not a good idea because it would alert the North Vietnamese.

McNamara then phoned President Johnson with news of the delay and suggested that he postpone his address until 10 and leave out the passage about air action now in progress. What, Johnson wanted to know, had delayed the attack? Briefing crews on the mission and loading designated ordnance, McNamara replied. The last aircraft would be off target at about midnight, Washington time. Johnson worried that a premature announcement would leave him vulnerable to charges that he tipped off the enemy to the impending actions, and he would "sure as hell hate to have some mother say, 'You announced it and my boy got killed.'" McNamara assured him there was little danger that would happen, and asked how late Johnson would be willing to hold off his statement. The president replied the 11 o'clock news, but wondered if he even had to make a statement. McNamara was emphatic that something needed to be said. The president walked a tightrope over the timing of his address. He had to avoid alerting the North Vietnamese to the air attacks but at the same time precede any announcement by Hanoi of the raids.

With still no word of any launch, McNamara contacted Sharp at 9:22 urging him to get the aircraft off their carriers, but to no avail. Again at 10:06 McNamara called, and Sharp told him that although he had received no word, he was sure that one outfit went up at 10. But, he said, *Constellation* was not going to launch its propeller aircraft until 1 A.M. EDT August 5 and its jet fighters at 2:30 A.M. The launches were delayed because the carrier could not get into position. "You got that, sir?" "Yes. My God," snapped McNamara, who told Sharp to get in touch with *Ticonderoga* "and make damn sure she got off." Forty minutes later McNamara tried again, with the same result. Sharp still had no word on any launch. Could not Sharp ask in the clear if the 10 o'clock thing had happened? The president wanted to go on the air at 11:15, "and he shouldn't go on unless he has a confirmation of a launch." Sharp said he was "needling them like mad" but the "circuit is a little jammed up or something."

Only ten minutes before the president was to go on national television, Sharp phoned McNamara to report that *Ticonderoga* had gotten its planes off fifty minutes earlier, at 10:30 EDT. They would be over target in one hour and fifty minutes. McNamara was confused. How could it take so long—2½ hours—to reach their targets? Sharp explained that the planes launched in two waves, slower ones first, and then formed up to make a coordinated attack. Still, the time interval between takeoff and attack surprised both Sharp and McNamara, who had assumed the time from first launch to actual strike would be about forty minutes to one hour. When McNamara phoned the White House at 11:25, the president was unable to take the call, so McNamara told McGeorge Bundy that the planes were airborne. Bundy replied that Johnson would speak in about ten minutes.

Sharp, however, had misunderstood the launch information. Only four propeller-driven A-1 Skyraiders had taken off, and they orbited the carrier until 11:15 before departing for their targets. *Ticonderoga* launched its jet aircraft between 12:16 and 12:23 August 5—that is, after the president addressed the nation and while McNamara was telling reporters at the Pentagon that naval aircraft from both carriers "have already conducted airstrikes against the North Vietnamese bases from which these PT-boats have operated." *Constellation*, as Sharp had told McNamara, launched its first aircraft at 1 A.M. on August 5, followed ninety minutes later by a second wave.

Ticonderoga's aircraft struck southern ports first, and three hours later *Constellation*'s pilots attacked northern targets. During the later raids, North Vietnamese anti-aircraft gunners shot down two U.S. aircraft, an A-1 Skyraider over the Loc Chau PT-boat base and an A-4 Skyhawk at Hon Gay, northeast of Haiphong. The Skyraider airman was killed, while the A-4 pilot, Lt. j.g. Everett Alvarez Jr., parachuted from his damaged aircraft and spent the next 8½ years in captivity in Hanoi.

Johnson had second thoughts about the two lost aircraft, but Bundy assured him there was no evidence that his public announcement had adversely affected the operations in any way. According to Bundy, North Vietnamese radar operators had picked up the carrier planes before Johnson spoke on national radio and television. Post-strike assessments, Bundy told Johnson, revealed there was no significant alert at the ports struck by the first attack from *Ticonderoga*. The loss of two planes occurred during *Constellation*'s attacks, which were hours later, long after the North Vietnamese went to full alert following the first attack.

On August 4, 1964, amid confusion, uncertainty, misinformation, and painfully slow communications, senior administration officials had to make a critical decision. One might speculate on why they made the one they did. After the August 2 attack in the Gulf of Tonkin, from the decks of *Maddox* to the halls of the Pentagon, everyone was on edge about the possibility of another North Vietnamese attack. Official Washington was predisposed to strike back given any future provocation. With those preconceptions, it became less important to question the accuracy of events on the night of August 4 than to ready a retaliatory strike. In brief, most attention and energy went into responding to, not assessing, what had happened.

Time constraints placed further pressure on decision makers. Any retaliation, they believed, had to be carried out right away to demonstrate U.S. resolve to North Vietnam and had to be clearly linked to the provocation to justify the response. Waiting several days to sort out the last detail of the August 4 action would blur any linkage and raise questions about the propriety of attacking well after the fact instead of at the time of the provocation. Once U.S. wire services began reporting the new attacks of August 4, there seemed even more reason for Johnson to act quickly.

Neither Washington nor Hanoi had been willing to blink. The administration stepped up OPLAN 34-A operations, Hanoi reacted by reinforcing its coastal naval units in the southern panhandle, the United States ordered a Desoto patrol, OPLAN 34-A raids continued, and North Vietnamese PT-boats attacked *Maddox* on August 2. Several intercepted North Vietnamese messages were ambiguous. The one McNamara cited as proof positive that an attack occurred may be a recap of the August 2 action intercepted during retransmission to another recipient. But the intercept that got Herrick's attention ordered North Vietnamese PT-boats and Swatows "to make ready for military operations" on the night of August 4. One may question whether "military operations" meant "attack," but the August 4 reference left prudent commanders like Herrick and Ogier little choice but to expect trouble in the Gulf that night.

Tandem events, one after the other in rapid sequence, produced a cumulative effect that made any single one of the interrelated and often confusing episodes less consequential than the aggregate picture, which in Washington was one of clear-cut North Vietnamese aggression. That of course is hindsight, a commodity that the civilians and military leaders making decisions on the afternoon and evening of August 4, 1964, could not possess.

EDWARD J. DREA is a regular *MHQ* contributor and the author of *In the Service of the Emperor: Essays on the Imperial Japanese Army* (Bison Books, 2003).

At a remote, often-rebuilt fort in northern England,
archaeologists have uncovered a treasure-trove of information on
Roman military life, much of it written on small wooden tablets.

Roman Soldiers'

by David G. Frye

OF ALL THE OUTPOSTS IN the Roman Empire, Vindolanda, in northern England, was most assuredly the wettest. Soaked by rains from above and springs from below, the auxiliary troops who manned Vindolanda learned to spread dried bracken, and sometimes straw and moss, over their floors to form a kind of barrier against the damp. This carpet may have protected their feet, but it could do nothing to prevent their timber barracks from rotting, and from A.D. 85 to 104, the men of the garrison were forced to rebuild their fort four times. Such work would hardly have daunted Roman soldiers, who

Written Record

were accustomed to building elaborate camps on each night of a march. And certainly none of these auxiliary troops could have imagined the extraordinary effect of their efforts. For those same soldiers who rebuilt Vindolanda with such tiresome frequency were also inadvertently creating one of the world's greatest archaeological treasures—and a priceless window into the life of the ordinary Roman soldier.

The soldiers stationed at Vindolanda occupied an outpost far from their homes and even farther from Rome. They were emblematic of a Roman army that had grown increasingly dependent on foreign recruits in the late first century. Most had probably never seen Rome, but nearly all had tasted action, and they arrived in Britain as battle-proven veterans.

The first troops to man Vindolanda were Tungrians—men from the tribe that gave its name to present-day Tongeren in Belgium. According to the Roman historian Tacitus, their ancestors had once crossed the Rhine River from Germany and displaced the fearsome Gauls. Since then, Tungrian cohorts had served admirably within the Roman army, waging fierce battles across the empire. During the Roman civil war of A.D. 69-70, rival emperors vied desperately for Tungrian support. At first Rome's Tungrian soldiers supported Vitellius in heavy fighting against his rival Otho. Later those same Tungrians joined the "German revolt" in favor of Vespasian. Once Vespasian had finally established stability, he ordered the Tungrians to Britain.

The Tungrians were joined there, and succeeded at Vindolanda, by Batavian troops who were, if anything, even more battle tested. Natives of what is now called Holland, the Batavians were, according to Tacitus, "foremost among all these [German] nations in valour." Unique among the empire's allies, the Batavians paid no taxes or tribute to Rome; their sole contribution consisted of tough fighting men, who took orders only from Batavian officers, even when fighting for Rome.

Over the years, Rome made heavy use of its Batavian auxiliaries. Batavian cavalry guarded the emperors, while crack Batavian infantry fought in Britain. In A.D. 69, the Roman general Aulus Vitellius used the veteran Batavian infantry to help him seize the throne in Italy. However, when Vitellius ordered his officers to conscript even more Batavian men, the tribe changed its allegiance and threw its support to his rival, Vespasian. In the months that followed, the Batavians proved to be some of Rome's toughest fighters—as well as her most treacherous.

In A.D. 70, Batavian troops came close to wrenching the northern world away from Rome. Led by their ambitious

Above right: A Roman aquilifer, or standard-bearer, comes ashore in Britain during Julius Caesar's 55 B.C. invasion of the island. Many of the Roman soldiers stationed at Vindolanda were natives of Batavia (in present-day Holland), which in A.D. 70 had rebelled against Rome. Right: The revolt's leader, Julius Civilis (with arm outstretched), meets with Roman commanders.

nobleman Julius Civilis, the Batavians lashed out against the empire when it was weakened by civil war. Despite bearing a name that suggests his family had possessed Roman citizenship for more than a century, Civilis forsook all Roman ways and undertook the barbarian vow that he would not cut his red-dyed hair until he had defeated a legion. This vow would not be in vain. At Vetera the Batavian commander forced two legions to surrender, but the Roman general Cerialis finally drove the rebels back and ransacked their homeland.

We do not know exactly how the rebellion ended—Tacitus' history breaks off at this crucial point—but we do know that the Batavians were exhausted from the struggle. Even before the decisive battles, they had sent a message to a legionary commander: "We have no quarrel with the Romans, for whom we have so often fought. Wearied with a protracted and fruitless service, we now long for our native land and for rest." They might as well have saved their breath. For the empire would allow the Batavians no rest, and sent them,

along with the Tungrians—who had joined their rebellion—to Britain.

Britain was, in the first century A.D., anything but the center of Western civilization. Indeed, it was as far-flung and dangerous a province as any within the Roman Empire. The island had missed out on the early, spectacular rise of civilization in the Mediterranean and still seemed a rather barbarous place to Julius Caesar when he first led Roman troops there in 55 B.C. Caesar lacked the resources to effect a permanent occupa-

tion of the island, and Britain would remain independent from Rome until the campaigns of Emperor Claudius, nearly one hundred years later. Even then, Rome found Britain a hard land to subdue. The British revolt under Queen Boudicca in A.D. 61 proved a bloody reversal, and the Roman invasion of the British island of Anglesey—where black-attired women with hair "like furies" waved torches as they stood alongside their soldiers and cursing druidic priests on the shore—terrified Roman troops with a vivid display of how wild and untamed Britain remained.

After the civil war of 69-70, much work remained to be done by the Roman military in Britain. In assigning Tungrian and Batavian troops to the province, Rome was sending some of its toughest cohorts. The assignment may also have reflected Rome's decision to station troops of questionable loyalty as far away as possible from their homelands, where they might tend to revolt or otherwise cause trouble.

One hint of that policy is found in the names of their commanders. The old Batavian aristocracy, which—like Julius Civilis—came from families whose Roman citizenship dated back to the days of Caesar, had been replaced, if not altogether eliminated. The new Batavian nobility—represented by its Vindolanda commanders—had received citizenship only after A.D. 70, when the Flavian emperors came to power. Indeed, one Batavian commander, Flavius Cerialis, may have been named for the very man who had crushed the Batavian revolt, Petillius Cerialis.

The Batavian cohorts, nearly decimated during the revolt of Civilis, would initially find little rest in Britain. During his campaigns into Scotland, the Roman governor Gnaeus Julius Agricola carefully husbanded his legions, sending forth his Tungrian and Batavian auxiliaries to do most of the dirty work. They served him well. At the Battle of Mons Graupius, the unconquered Britons rained volleys of darts upon Agricola's troops until he ordered the charge of three Batavian and two Tungrian cohorts.

The Britons, armed with unwieldy swords and shields, could not stand up to the close-fighting tactics of these hardened warriors, who slashed through their foes as they advanced up a hill. Their work was deadly. According to Tacitus: "The open plain presented an awful and hideous spectacle. Our men pursued, wounded, made prisoners of the fugitives only to slaughter them when others fell in their way....Everywhere there lay scattered arms, corpses, and mangled limbs, and the earth reeked with blood." At the end of the battle, some ten thousand Britons lay slaughtered, against only 360 Roman deaths.

The Tungrians and Batavians had thus proven themselves admirably against the Caledonian Britons of what is now Scotland. It was therefore not surprising that the Romans should assign these cohorts to guard the northernmost part of the empire. What does come as some surprise is that the boundary they came to guard fell well short of Agricola's line of conquests. For reasons that have never been clear, the empire elected not to occupy Scotland but to create a boundary somewhat south of where Agricola had temporarily extended the empire. The Romans opted for a border that stretched across the narrowest part of the island of Britain, ensuring that the defensive line would be as short as possible. Batavians and Tungrians were dispersed along the boundary at several key points, including Vindolanda. They established their presence there in the typical Roman way: by building a fort.

ROMAN ARMIES were prodigious fort-builders. On the march, they built highly organized camps, complete with streets, to protect them from nighttime ambush. When they settled down to defend a particular area, they constructed more permanent forts along the same pattern. A typical Roman fort was neatly divided by a rectangular grid of streets. Toward the center lay two large buildings, the *praetoria* (commander's residence) and *principia* (headquarters). Barracks made up much of

the rest of the complex but were supplemented by a hospital, granaries, bathhouses and, in the larger legionary fortresses, even amphitheaters.

Vindolanda lacked the scale of the more elaborate legionary fortresses. It was designed to house a cohort, a smaller military unit (traditionally around 480 men) only about a tenth the size of a legion. Not surprisingly, then, the Tungrians and Batavians did not bother with anything as ambitious as an amphitheater. However, they did provide for the creature comfort of heated baths.

They built their fort on green, spring-fed land near what would, within a few decades, become the site of Hadrian's Wall. There was nothing particularly defensible about the site. Had defense been a primary consideration, the Romans could have built on a nearby hill to the east—the location, in fact, of an earlier Celtic hill fort—but they chose not to. The decision was in keeping with standard Roman tactics; imperial troops did not fight from behind walls, except during extreme emergencies. They lived behind the walls but preferred to seek battle in open fields. Thus the hill was used only for a signal tower and for supplies of rock, which the soldiers used to build their roads.

The first forts constructed at Vindolanda were made of timber, which could not long withstand the humid conditions of northern England. Consequently, it became customary to tear down the buildings and begin anew every time a new cohort came to man the outpost. When forced to rebuild a fort, the soldiers carefully inspected their old uniforms and equipment, jettisoning anything that was worn out or no longer useful. They would then level the older structures, salvaging any useful wood and packing turf or clay over the debris to create a level building surface. What no Tungrian or Batavian could possibly have realized was that the weight of the new structures would compact the turf and clay into a layer of soil so dense that it could not support the bacteria that ordinarily break down organic materials.

Not until 1973 did archaeologists work-

DAVID FRYE

ing at Vindolanda fully realize what an extraordinary collection lay underneath the wet topsoil. They had already discovered leathers and textiles in a remarkable state of preservation (shoes and sandals so well preserved that the imprints of feet remained, goatskin tent panels still bearing traces of a waterproofing sheen), but when Robin Birley spotted writing on a tiny sliver of wood, he was thunderstruck. Very little ink writing had survived anywhere from the Roman era, and Birley could not at first be sure that what he had found was even Roman at all. To make matters worse, within minutes the treasured text began to fade away before

his eyes, like some ancient ghost writing. Fortunately, infrared photography managed to recapture the text, and historians soon realized that the writing was not only Roman but also an exciting new source on the Roman military.

The clay of Vindolanda proved to contain a virtual library of writing tablets,

replete with records and even correspondence from the Tungrians and Batavians. The tablets were usually fragmented and always difficult to read, but as more and more have been pulled from the clay, scholars have managed to develop an unusually realistic picture of military life on the British frontier. From the start, historians learned that the "barbarian" Tungrian and Batavian soldiery were surprisingly literate. They wrote letters, and they did so in the language of the Roman military, Latin.

In the first century A.D., Roman soldiers had never heard of paper (except for Egyptian papyrus, which would have

Far left: This aerial view gives a good idea of the size of Vindolanda. Roman soldiers constructed several forts on the site, each on top of the remains of the others. The tablets excavated there date from about A.D. 85-130, when the walls were built of timber. The rectangular outline of a later fort is visible in this photograph. Within its stone walls are the remains of the fort prefect's house (praetoria) and the headquarters (principia). Located just south of Scotland, Vindolanda was an outpost along Roman Britain's frontier. Within fifty years of its founding, Hadrian's Wall (opposite inset) was built a few miles to the north. Above: A bathhouse, the floor of which rested on pillars, was the early fort's only building constructed of stone. Left: Robin Birley, director of excavations at Vindolanda, discovered the first wooden tablets.

been unavailable in Britain), so they made do with other media. Sometimes they made reusable writing surfaces by hollowing out the centers of wooden tablets and filling them with wax. Scribes using styluses could scratch letters into this wax, which could easily be erased and written over (letters showed up white against the black wax). Vindolanda's archaeologists have found scores of these so-called stylus tablets, but in every case so far the wax has disappeared, taking with it the text. Fortunately, most of Vindolanda's soldiers seem to have preferred writing in ink. By slicing alder and birch woods into thin slivers, the troops could create postcard-size tablets or, if a longer document was required, folded sheets. It is the ink writings that have survived in legible form.

THE VINDOLANDA tablets quickly dispelled many prevailing images of a shaggy, disorganized Roman army made barbarous by its growing dependence on foreign troops. Close to half of all the writing tablets represent official documents of some sort, and they reveal that the Roman army—even at the northernmost tip of the empire— was a resolutely bureaucratic animal. Some things, it seems, never change.

Bureaucratic documents were no more interesting nineteen centuries ago than they are today, but they do reveal Rome's insistence on precision and information. Even Rome's barbarian auxiliaries seem to have conducted daily inspections of men and equipment and com-

mitted the results to writing. One remarkable report—the only one of its kind ever recovered from the Roman Empire—enumerates the entire garrison, putting the cohort's strength at some 752 men (a figure unnaturally large for a cohort, although it may have been in the process of being doubled). Of that 752, we learn that fully 456 men were absent, although generally accounted for. Three hundred thirty-seven of the absent had been deployed at a nearby fort called Coria (present-day Corbridge). Another substantial detachment (146 men) had been assigned to help guard the commander of the legion in York. Only 296 men actually remained at Vindolanda, and of those, thirty-one were sick, wounded, or suffering from what is believed to have been pink eye.

Other surviving documents include duty rosters, which listed the daily tasks

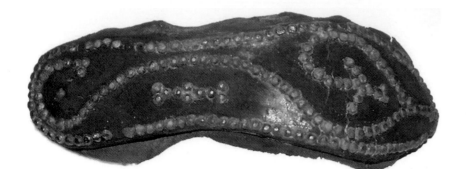

In addition to tablets, Vindolanda's dense soil preserved other priceless artifacts that offer insight into daily Roman life. The archaeological finds include remarkably well-preserved footwear, such as a woman's shoe featuring a decorative pattern of hobnails (above left), a soldier's marching boot (above right), and the only Roman sock ever discovered (right).

of Vindolanda's soldiers. These tasks underscore the fact that a soldier's life was not all iron and glory. Indeed, the same fearsome cohorts whose predecessors had once thrown a scare into the empire now settled into a rather mundane routine. One duty roster recorded 343 soldiers "in the workshops." Of those, some were assigned to make shoes, others to build a bathhouse, still others to dig clay, work at the kilns, repair tents, collect rubble, assist in plastering, load wagons—everything, it seems, but fight. There are duty rosters showing soldiers building a residence, burning stone to make lime, and preparing wattle for fences, but none so far have mentioned battle.

Like modern soldiers, first-century Roman auxiliaries must have longed for any relief from these chores, and no small number of the tablets follow a predictable format: "I ask, my lord Cerialis, that you consider me a worthy person to grant leave." Or, "I ask that you consider me a worthy person to whom to grant leave at Ulucium." Or, "I, Messicus...ask, my lord, that you consider me a worthy person to grant leave at Coria," and so forth. It is difficult to say exactly what wonders might have awaited a furloughed soldier at nearby Coria (a woman, perhaps?), but one supposes that anything would beat collecting clay for wattle fences.

For all its bureaucracy, the Roman army, at least at Vindolanda, does not exactly present a picture of smooth efficiency. For example, the army built roads to facilitate supply and troop movement, but in one letter a certain Octavius fretted that he might not be able to supply Vindolanda while the roads were in such a sorry state. Indeed, archaeologists at Vindolanda snicker a little when they hear modern historians wax enthusiastic on the vaunted roads of Rome—roads reputedly so deeply and permanently laid that they have never worn out. In their neck of the woods, at Vindolanda, the Roman "roads" are little better than goat paths.

Bad roads were not the only obstacle that could stymie the army. Human inefficiency could also get in the way. In one fragmentary letter, we glimpse a snafu that had developed in regard to a work assignment. Apparently a unit led by Vocontius had been detailed to transport stone. Vocontius, however, had developed his own perspective on how the stone should be handled, and he was refusing to budge unless he be allowed to sort the stone into the wagons his way.

We do not find out what happened to Vocontius as a result of his apparent disobedience, but we do know that military justice could be severe at Vindolanda. In one instance, a visiting trader seems to have fallen afoul of the law:

As befits an honest man, I implore your majesty not to allow me, an innocent man, to be beaten with rods, my lord, inasmuch as I was unable to complain to the prefect because he was detained by ill health. I have complained in vain to the beneficarius and the rest of the centurions of his unit. Accordingly, I implore your mercifulness not to allow me, a man from overseas and an innocent one, about whose good faith you may enquire, to be bloodied by rods as if I had committed a crime.

Bloody rods, indeed—if this was the army's way of dealing with dishonest traders, one shudders to imagine what sort of discipline awaited the unnamed deserters referred to in the tablets!

Whatever the fate of the "innocent" man above, it is clear that civilians swarmed to the garrison at Vindolanda. For many, the presence of a cohort there represented a substantial business opportunity. Several of the tablets deal with private transactions between soldiers and traders. In the Roman world, towns maintained "public books" to keep track of transactions, loans, and even gifts, and it may well be that frontier forts had a similar process for registering contracts. At any rate, the tablets reveal a lively exchange between the garrison and its surroundings. We see soldiers buying and selling wheat, ox hides, axles, hubs, lumber, and a host of other commodities. What emerges is less a picture of an isolated fort in a hostile land than of an outpost that quickly merged with the local economy.

Some soldiers became downright entrepreneurial. One letter, found in the old barracks, dealt with a host of ventures being carried out by two men named Octavius and Candidus. Their enterprise did not always run smoothly, as this letter suggests: "I have several times written to you that I have bought about five thousand modii of ears of grain, on account of which I need cash. Unless you send me some cash, at least five thousand denarii, the result will be that I shall lose what I have laid out as a deposit, about three hundred denarii, and I shall be embarrassed."

Octavius had made a sizable investment in grain, but various tablets make clear that Vindolanda's soldiers did not live on bread alone. They consumed a variety of meats and poultries, including venison, pork, and chicken, and acquired carbohydrates from both barley and wheat flour. Apples, grapes, beans, and nuts are mentioned, but, if the documents are any indication, the soldiers' diet could have used more fruits and vegetables. The discriminating Tungrian gourmand could also purchase anise, pepper, and mustard for spices, as well as alum for pickling.

Eventually a small military settlement, a *vicus*, grew up around the fort. We can only imagine what sort of people lived there—traders, servants, day laborers, almost certainly prostitutes—but such settlements were common at forts throughout the empire.

WITHIN THE FORT, the soldiers were not entirely divorced from civilian life, but their experience varied according to rank. For the common foot soldier, this was the army. He lived in barracks, in tight quarters with other men of his rank. The result for many was a lifelong bond of friendship.

Several of the tablets reveal the warm bond that existed between soldiers who had once shared the cramped barracks of

While Roman Samian pottery is found throughout Britain in broken pieces, archaeologists at Vindolanda have discovered hoards of the utilitarian stoneware, much of it in virtually pristine condition.

Vindolanda. One was a letter from London that read:

Chrauttius to Veldeius, his brother and old messmate, very many greetings. And I ask you, brother Veldeius—I am surprised that you have written nothing back to me for such a long time—whether you have heard anything from our elders, or about —, in which unit he is; and greet him from me in my words, and Virilis the veterinarian. Ask Virilis whether you may send through one of our friends the pair of shears which he promised me in exchange for money. And I ask you, brother Virilis, to greet from me our sister Thuttena. Write back to us how Velbuteius is. It is my wish that you enjoy the best of fortune. Farewell.

Packages from home have always been welcome in the military, and the garrison at Vindolanda was no exception. The following letter accompanied a priceless care gift: "I have sent you…pairs of socks from Sattua, two pairs of sandals, and two pairs of underpants….Greet…[fragments of names], Tetricus and all your messmates with whom I hope that you live in the greatest good fortune." Another soldier wrote, "A friend sent me fifty oysters from Cordovi."

In general, the letters from the commander's household reveal a lifestyle that differed dramatically from that of the ordinary barracks dweller. Roman commanders were almost never professional soldiers. The legions that conquered much of the world were led by politicians who regarded legionary command as an obligatory step in a political career. Even the position of second-in-command devolved upon an aspiring young member of the senatorial class, usually no older than twenty, with no military experience.

Rome's indifference to the military qualifications of its officers also prevailed at the cohort level. Cohorts were headed by prefects drawn from the empire's wealthy equestrian class, and the Vindolanda tablets confirm that these part-time officers regarded military command as a temporary inconvenience. One Vindolanda prefect even wrote, "…furnish me with friends that thanks to you I may be able to enjoy a pleasant period of military service."

LIFE WAS HARDLY opulent at Vindolanda, but it should not have been too terribly hard on these commanders. The prefects not only enjoyed a private residence but also brought along their families to see them through

and he may even have brought a small library with him. At least one tablet contains a poorly copied line from Virgil's *Aeneid*. The *Aeneid* was so widely used for writing exercises that one is tempted to imagine the prefect's children dutifully copying the verse, their education unimpeded by their father's temporary assignment to the end of the empire.

As if family alone did not provide sufficient comfort, Vindolanda's commanders also brought their servants with them. Several tablets attest to the prefect's slaves, and at least one represents a communication from one slave to another.

beer and sixteen of wine. On the following day, consumption swelled to more than twenty-five liters of beer, and thirty liters of various wines. Vindolanda's commander was not going to let the little matter of a military command get in the way of his enjoyment of the good life.

It comes as some relief, then, to find that the enlisted men were not altogether forced to endure a life of hardship. One tablet preserves a request to the prefect, ostensibly for orders, although the end of the letter perhaps reveals its true purpose: "Masculus to Cerialis his king, greetings. Please, my lord, give instructions on what you want us to do tomorrow. Are we all to return with the standard or just half of us?…My fellow soldiers have no beer. Please order some to be sent."

It is at least possible that Masculus and his men had developed their thirst while battling Rome's enemies, but realistically we have no reason to make such an assumption. In fact, out of all the tablets so far unearthed, only one has made concrete reference to fighting, and it reads more like an intelligence report than a battle summary: "The Britons are unprotected by armor. There are very many cavalry. The cavalry do not use swords, nor do the wretched Britons mount in order to throw javelins."

The great majority of the writings uncovered pertain to soldier life, but one extraordinary letter is from the wife of a neighboring fort's prefect to the wife of Vindolanda's prefect: "I send you warm invitation to come to us on September 11th for my birthday celebrations to make my day more enjoyable by your presence.…I will expect you, sister."

their tedious assignment in northern Britain. Archaeologists have found both women's and children's shoes buried in the clay of Vindolanda, and these noncombatants left their mark on the tablets as well. One of the most extraordinary of all the Vindolanda letters was sent from the wife of Corbridge's prefect to the wife of Vindolanda's prefect: "I send you warm invitation to come to us on September 11th for my birthday celebrations to make my day more enjoyable by your presence. Give my greetings to your Cerialis. My Aelius greets you and your sons. I will expect you, sister." It is a birthday party invitation, and not the only communication between the "first ladies" of these two neighboring forts. They actually carried on a blithe intercourse, freely visiting one another as well.

The reference to sons in the party invitation indicates that the prefect Cerialis had set up house at Vindolanda. His inventories reveal a substantial collection of tableware, lamps, and clothes,

In it, a servant refers to the upcoming celebration of the Saturnalia. This was the day when ordinary class roles were reversed, and masters served their slaves. It was one of the wilder Roman celebrations, comparable to the medieval Feast of Fools, and it was by no means the only festival kept at Vindolanda.

At the commander's residence, if not throughout the garrison, festivals were a serious business. One tablet accounts for some of the foodstuffs purchased for the prefect's household over a week in June, which included a festival of the goddess Fortuna. The list includes substantial quantities of barley, vinegar, fish sauce, and pork fat, but otherwise it concerned itself almost entirely with the consumption of alcohol: some Celtic beer on the nineteenth, followed by seventeen more liters of beer on the twentieth, and probably another seventeen liters on the next day. The twenty-second saw the purchase of Massic wine, supplemented on the twenty-third by twenty-six more liters of

Thus, Vindolanda's tablets have forced historians to rethink many long-accepted notions of the Roman military. Images of jackbooted legions, living on hardtack while they "made a desert and called it peace," or of long-haired barbarians fighting for Rome without becoming Roman somehow just do not fit the evidence. What we find in the Vindolanda tablets is sometimes shockingly unromantic—a sock-wearing, bath-taking, beer-guzzling, wattle-collecting, record-keeping, letter-writing collection of soldiers who may well have exemplified the Roman army of the late first century. The Vindolanda troops had it tougher than some, to be sure, and perhaps better than others, but they held their wet ground for Rome and in so doing did their small part to maintain the greatest empire of the ancient world.

DAVID G. FRYE is an associate professor of history at Eastern Connecticut State University.

FIGHTING WORDS

Terms from Military History

by Christine Ammer

Like many others, I always thought **D-Day** simply represented an alliteration, like H-hour, but apparently that is not necessarily true. The "D" in D-Day may, some think, as I did, stand for "day." However, the French maintained it stood for "disembarkation," which some others call "debarkation," and indeed the term originally was a code designation for the U.S. offensive at St. Mihiel during World War I. Others believe that it stood for "day of decision." According to lexicographer Robert Hendrickson, all these interpretations are possibilities, but when someone wrote to General Dwight D. Eisenhower in 1964 to ask for a definite answer, his assistant, Brig. Gen. Robert Schultz, replied, "General Eisenhower [advised] that any amphibious operation has a 'departed date,' and hence the shortening D-Day was used." And this, of course, is what the largest amphibious attack known to history has been called. Moreover, in civilian terms, the designation has been transferred to any important day or occasion (for example, "May 1 is D-day, when we turn the management over to the new CEO").

D-Day, June 6, 1944, might never have happened if the Allies had not cracked the Germans' codes. Deciphering coded intelligence during wartime dates back to Napoleon's day but reached new heights when cryptographers worked round the clock in Great Britain and figured out exactly how to decode Nazi radio messages. The fact that the Germans were quite confused as to just where an Allied landing in France might take place was enormously helpful to the Allied invasion force. And the term **crack the code** has been used ever since for solving a difficult problem or mystery.

The official designation for the Allied invasion was **Operation Overlord**. The assault involved more than one million ground troops, escorted across the English Channel by battleships, cruisers, and destroyers. A general term applied to them was **task force**, which had originated in 1942 with the amphibious landings in North Africa and came to be used in the military for a temporary force formed to carry out a specific mission. This expression, too, carried over to postwar peacetime, where it designates a group formed to investigate or solve a particular problem. President John F. Kennedy was particularly fond of the term and set up task forces for foreign aid and numerous other issues.

A crucial factor was the U.S. air force, with its heavy bombardment of German coastal defenses and French railroads, followed by the descent of British and American paratroopers behind the German lines. When troops assaulted the beaches, more than two thousand bombers and 171 squadrons of fighters aided the attack.

The ground forces were armed with, among other weapons, **bazookas**, tubular anti-tank rocket launchers used since 1943. Operated by two men, one who loaded it and another who fired it and carried it on his shoulder, it supposedly could destroy any enemy tank. The bazooka is about four feet long and less than three inches in diameter. Its curious name came from its resemblance to a comedian's musical instrument, popularized by radio celebrity Bob Burns in the 1930s. Burns claimed to have invented the instrument, first by blowing into a section of gas pipe and then sliding a rolled sheet of music in and out of one end, similar to a trombone's slide. Its comical sound led him to embellish it with a second metal pipe to slide in and out of the first, and to add a funnel on one end. Burns himself had enlisted in the U.S. Marine Corps during World War I, went overseas, and later became leader of the corps' jazz band in Europe, which actually included a bazooka. It is not known who first named the weapon for the instrument, but the name has stuck.

The German army had installed itself for all-out defense, and the Normandy terrain was bristling with gun emplacements, mines, and hedgerows, mounds of earth topped with thick bushes, which bounded the countryside's many small fields. The hedgerows presented a serious threat, for Germans hiding behind them could simply pick off the invading soldiers as they crawled over them and crossed the fields. The problem was solved by Sergeant Curtis G. Culin of the 102nd Cavalry, who devised an attachment for tanks called **rhino horns**. This steel mechanism consisted of four pieces of iron sharpened at one end and welded to a steel plate attached to the front of the tank, making it resemble a rhinoceros. It enabled the tank to tear holes through the earthen hedgerows.

The Allies' air support included low-flying planes that strafed the enemy. Such missions were called **rhubarb**, and their fliers **rhubarb pilots**, because they flew so low that they allegedly returned to base with pieces of rhubarb stuck to their planes.

The Allied advance in Normandy was aided by the French **underground**, the civilian resistance movement that worked throughout the war to overthrow the occupying Axis power. One of the earliest uses of this term for a secret opposition to established powers was the mid-nineteenth-century Underground Railroad whereby slaves escaped from the South to the North. But it was revived during World War II for the Belgian and French resistance and has been associated with it ever since. The term has subsequently been used for various nonconformist enterprises, not necessarily secret or subversive. Thus we speak of an **underground newspaper** that caters to avant-garde arts, or an **underground economy** that operates outside the conventional banking system. Another name for the French underground was **maquis**, originally denoting a dense growth of small trees and shrubs and transferred to the resistance, who figuratively fought from such concealment.

CHRISTINE AMMER's latest word book is *The Facts on File Dictionary of Clichés* (2001).

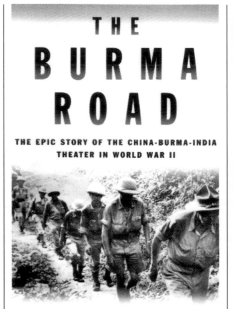

Donovan Webster, *The Burma Road* (Farrar, Straus and Giroux, 2003), $25.

ALTHOUGH IT HAS some shortcomings, Donovan Webster's well-researched, beautifully written account of the China-Burma-India (CBI) Theater during World War II is a superb piece of military history. His formula for book writing is simple and highly effective: Study all the best sources on the subject, personally inspect the setting of the story, interview as many veterans as possible, and write in an entertaining and informative style.

Webster traveled thousands of miles and interviewed scores of battle participants—Japanese, Americans, Kachin tribesmen, and anyone else who could provide firsthand accounts of the fighting, brutality, destruction, and dying that took place in Burma from 1942 to '45. He has also carefully used relevant memoirs, official histories, and studies of CBI battles and campaigns. The author writes with occasional eloquence, skillfully incorporating vivid de-scriptions from those who were there.

The Burma Road describes many people, events, and places, but it has twin themes: the character, actions, and thinking of one man—General Joseph W. Stilwell—and the design, construction, and effect of the Burma Road and the connecting Ledo Road on the war, the people who built it, and those who depended on these tortuous and vital paths.

Webster gives Stilwell, commander of U.S. and Chinese forces in the theater and one of the most fascinating figures in American military history, all the attention that the somewhat unfortunate general richly deserves. The author's description of "Vinegar Joe" borrows much from Barbara Tuchman's *Stilwell and the American Experience in China, 1911-45*, and rightly so. Some of Tuchman's three-decade-old writing about Stilwell's colorfulness, acid personality, and intense practicality bears repeating. The story of the Burma and Ledo Roads is revealed as a tale of great sacrifice, determination, and ingenuity. Webster also describes what the roads are like today.

The Burma Road has some relevance to today's military affairs. In the 1940s, the ability of the United States to safeguard its interests and succeed in its policies was in some cases largely dependent on the effectiveness of indigenous forces. Keeping China and India in the war and providing bases from which forces could strike Japanese military targets and Japan itself were of great importance to Washington. But there was nothing easy in the doing. The U.S. Army chief of staff, General George C. Marshall, described the task as "the most impossible job of the war." Stilwell's task fifty years ago has many similarities with our own present-day policies and programs in the endeavor to persuade and aid other countries to join us in defeating terrorist organizations and transform those nations that might support terrorism. The keys to American and British success in the 1940s in aiding and persuading would-be allies were negotiating talent, the ability to compromise, the patience to endure seemingly endless frustration, and the will to learn the ways of mystifying foreign cultures. What worked in Asia during World War II may shed light on Washington's current trials.

The book's weaknesses are mostly mechanical. There are no chapter titles to provide a browsing prospective buyer with a quick clue as to what the book does or does not address. Having only numbers to discriminate between chapters also deprives readers from getting a "heads up" and a mind-set for what is about to come. The book has endnotes but no indication within the text that a particular quote or assertion has a reference. The reader has to assume there is an endnote, remember the page number of the text, go to the back of the book, and see if there is a source for the quote or item in question.

Finally, Webster uses too many flash-

backs. A digression within a digression is annoying, and jumping from one scene or subject to another can jolt the reader.

These shortcomings, however, are minor. Some readers may prefer a clean text devoid of endnote indicators, the lack of a table of contents, and relentless TV-like moves from one subject to another. Nevertheless, the quality of the book is high. The language used, the previously unpublished veterans' stories, and the vibrant verbal imagery is well worth the price of *The Burma Road*.

Rod Paschall

Peter Huchthausen, *America's Splendid Little Wars* (Viking, 2003), $25.95.

JUST AS QUEEN VICTORIA'S reign was nowhere near as peaceful as is often supposed—there were little wars all over the British empire—so the final decades of the last century, a period in which the United States was militarily supreme, were marked by U.S. participation in a number of brush-fire conflicts. In this book Peter Huchthausen, a retired naval officer, analyzes some of the episodes of the period between 1975 and 2000, including President Jimmy Carter's ill-fated attempt to rescue American hostages from Iran, the U.S. invasions of Grenada and Panama, President Ronald Reagan's retaliatory attacks against Libya in 1986, the 1991 Gulf War, and the U.S.-led interventions in Bosnia and Kosovo.

The author's prose is tedious, but he has done his homework. In his discussion of the first Gulf War, for instance, he includes a brief history of the Kurdish people that is as much as many of us will require. The chapters on Bosnia and Kosovo—areas with which Huchthausen is apparently especially familiar—provide a useful summary of NATO's half-hearted efforts to slow the Serb-led ethnic cleansing in the Balkans.

Other failed interventions that the author considers are the sacrifice of 241 U.S. Marines in one terrorist attack in Lebanon in 1983 and President Bill Clinton's costly humanitarian intervention in Somalia. Of that operation, the author writes, U.S. Special Forces "lost the fight in the streets of Mogadishu" to a mob armed with knives and small arms.

He also notes that no satisfactory charts or beach studies of Somalia were available to American forces and that coordination between U.S. elements involved in the operation was notably poor. According to Huchthausen, while U.S. Rangers stalked one Somalian warlord, the U.S. government opened secret negotiations with him without notifying commanders in the field.

President Reagan's punitive attacks on Libya in 1986, the author says, indicated "that if aircraft carriers and land-based strike aircraft were available nearby, the United States could use its technological superiority to carry out attacks with few losses." Huchthausen goes on to argue that as a result of the U.S. raids Libyan leader Mohammar Qaddafi's "overt support of terror attacks ceased." Nevertheless, Libyan agents would destroy Pan Am Flight 103 two years later in one of the most flagrant terrorist attacks of this period.

The author calls the 1989 incursion into Panama to capture the notorious President Manuel Noriega a rare instance of a U.S. invasion of a country in order to capture its leader. The invasion plan was complex, but the author concludes that "its execution finally showed that the American armed forces were incorporating all the lessons learned…since the end of the Vietnam War."

Information security problems have arisen in all of America's recent wars. Whereas excessive secrecy complicated the invasion of Panama, it crippled the Iran hostage rescue. According to Huchthausen, most of the navy was kept in the dark about the importance of the mission, and as a result the rescue team was supplied with Sea Stallion helicopters, which were notorious for their poor maintenance records.

On the other hand, the very scale of the first Gulf War made such secrecy impractical. The author notes how TV crews were invited to film the arrival of giant air force transports in Saudi Arabia, and suggests that the buildup had an effect on the Iraqi psyche. "Televised news of the massive movement of men and machines enhanced the psychological message" of the power of the American-led coalition.

Where the United States is involved in peacekeeping, usually in concert with other powers, the desire to keep casualties to a minimum becomes paramount. Washington's preference for standoff, push-button warfare was pronounced during the intervention in Kosovo. There, to minimize losses, air attacks on Serb targets were limited to altitudes above ten thousand feet, and as a result the bombing had little effect on the ground.

The author believes that most of the failed ventures of the late twentieth century foundered because of policy shortcomings rather than poor military execution. Successful operations such as Grenada, Panama, and the first Gulf War, he believes, grew out of "an overall national policy that either was already in force at the time of the action or had been formed just prior to it." As we have learned in Iraq, however, one can have a highly successful military operation in support of a policy whose wisdom is open to question.

Although *America's Splendid Little Wars* is a solid account of U.S. military operations in the modern era, readers in search of a broader perspective may prefer Max Boot's *The Savage Wars of Peace*.

John M. Taylor

Bruce P. Gleason *explores the colorful history of horse-mounted military musicians, including side drummers and oboe players (right), both on the battlefield and parade ground. As one sixteenth-century veteran of Europe's religious wars wrote, "The sound of drums and trumpets animates the soul of man, and even horses receive emotion from it and become more superb and furious."*

• *Barry S. Strauss*, whose latest book is *The Battle of Salamis*, recounts the classic holding action in 480 B.C. that preceded the great Salamis naval clash. At the Greek mountain pass of Thermopylae, fewer than eight thousand Greeks, spearheaded by an elite unit of three hundred Spartans, gave a savage beating to a Persian army that outnumbered them by a ratio of perhaps 20-to-1.

• On July 15, 1839, one of the most audacious acts in the history of the U.S. Navy occurred when Lieutenant Charles Wilkes, commander of the sloop-of-war *Vincennes*, promoted himself to captain and then gave himself the honorary rank of commodore of the U.S. Exploring Expedition. According to *Nathaniel Philbrick*, what followed over the next three years was a voyage of unprecedented discovery and a tale of unbridled ego and stunning managerial incompetence.

• *Andrew McGregor* recounts France's hard 1880s campaign to conquer Tonkin (present-day northern Vietnam), which featured no-holds-barred warfare with Chinese regulars and semi-official brigands, known as the "Black Flags."

• General James A. Van Fleet faced many challenges during his long military career, including leading his regiment ashore on D-Day and advising government forces during Greece's war against Communist rebels. As *Allan R. Millet* explains, however, one his most difficult and rewarding assignments was helping to reform and expand the battered and disorganized army of the Republic of Korea during the Korean War.

COURTESY OF BRUCE P. GLEASON

Far left: World War I ace Eddie Rickenbacker had a string of remarkable experiences during World War II, according to Robert L. O'Connell. *Besides being stranded on a raft in the middle of the Pacific, "Captain Eddie" made an unauthorized trip to Moscow.* Steven E. Woodworth *recounts Ulysses S. Grant's feud with his most difficult subordinate, ambitious Maj. Gen. John A. McClernand (left), who was never above undercutting a superior officer.*

ABOVE LEFT: NATIONAL ARCHIVES; ABOVE RIGHT: *PHOTOGRAPHIC HISTORY OF THE CIVIL WAR*

IMPORTANT NOTICE

Articles in this listing of *MHQ* BACK ISSUES which relate to stories in the current issue of *MHQ* are highlighted in color.

For a complete listing of back issues or to order online: www.TheHistoryNetShop.com • or call: 800-358-6327 (U.S. & Canada)

THE QUARTERLY JOURNAL OF MILITARY HISTORY, PO Box 60, Kingstree, SC 29556

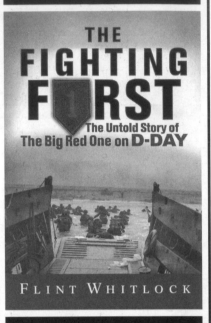
For a complete listing of back issues or to order online: www.TheHistoryNetShop.com • or call: 800-358-6327 (U.S. & Canada)

THE QUARTERLY JOURNAL OF MILITARY HISTORY, PO Box 60, Kingstree, SC 29556

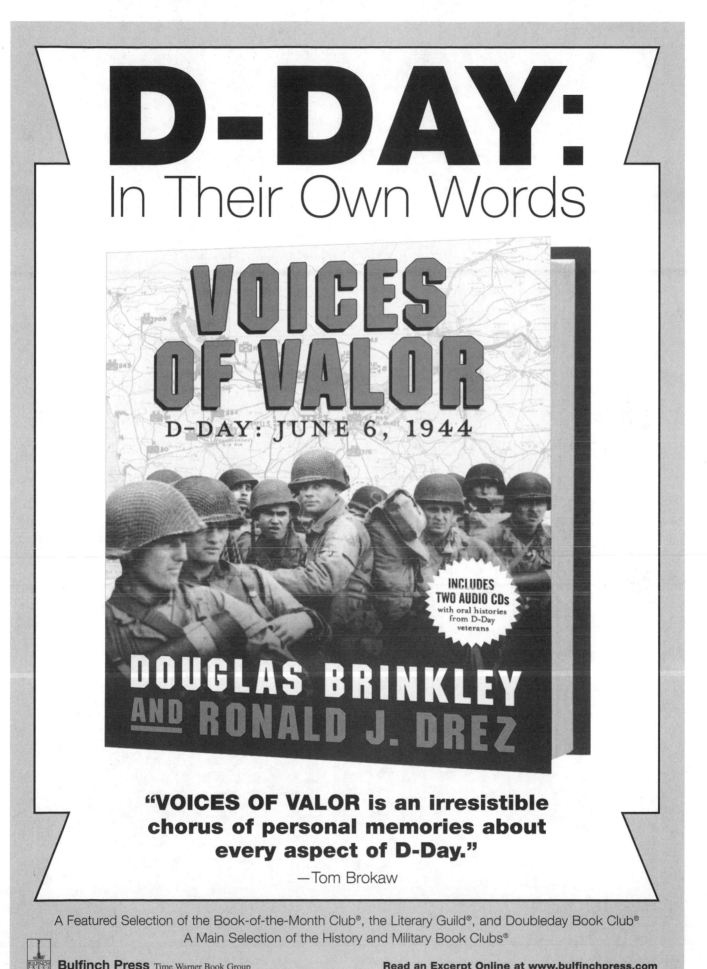